SURVIVING ALIEN
CONTACT AND ABDUCTION

SEAN T. PAGE

ROSEN
PUBLISHING

THIS EDITION PUBLISHED IN 2017 BY

THE ROSEN PUBLISHING GROUP, INC.
29 EAST 21ST STREET
NEW YORK, NY 10010

LIBRARY OF CONGRESS CATALOGING-IN-PUBLICATION DATA

NAMES: PAGE, SEAN T., AUTHOR.
TITLE: SURVIVING ALIEN CONTACT AND ABDUCTION / SEAN T. PAGE.
DESCRIPTION: NEW YORK, NY : ROSEN PUBLISHING GROUP, INC., C
2017. | SERIES: SURVIVING ALIEN CONTACT AND WARFARE | INCLUDES
BIBLIOGRAPHICAL REFERENCES AND INDEX.
IDENTIFIERS: LCCN 2016035783| ISBN 9781499465266 (LIBRARY BOUND) | ISBN
 9781499465259 (6 PACK) | ISBN 9781499465242 (PBK.)
SUBJECTS: LCSH: HUMAN-ALIEN ENCOUNTERS. | ALIEN ABDUCTION. |
SURVIVAL.
CLASSIFICATION: LCC BF2050 .P34 2017 | DDC 001.942--DC23
LC RECORD AVAILABLE AT HTTPS://LCCN.LOC.GOV/2016035783

MANUFACTURED IN CHINA

ORIGINALLY PUBLISHED IN ENGLISH BY HAYNES PUBLISHING UNDER THE TITLE: *ALIEN INVASION
MANUAL* © SEAN T. PAGE 2014.

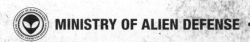

MINISTRY OF ALIEN DEFENSE

CONTENTS

A HISTORY OF ALIEN CONTACT 4

PRE-HISTORY (UP TO 1939) 6
THE MODERN ERA (1939–80) 8
AREA 51 (DREAMLAND) 10
THE BATTLE OF DULCE AIRBASE 12
THE POST–ROSWELL ERA (1980 ONWARDS) 14

ALIEN CONTACT AND ABDUCTION 16

FIRST-CONTACT PROTOCOLS 18
ALIENS AND THE LAW 20
ALIEN ABDUCTIONS 22
EYEWITNESS ACCOUNTS 24
ALIEN IMPLANTS 26
CATTLE MUTILATION 28

BECOMING AN ET PREPPER 30

GETTING THE LOOK 32
HOMEMADE PROTECTION 34
PREPPING FOR FAMILIES 36
ET PREPPER PRODUCTS 38
HOME DEFENSE 40
ABDUCTION PROOFING THE HOME 42
THE PERFECT ALIEN INVASION BUNKER 44

GLOSSARY 46
FOR MORE INFORMATION 47
FOR FURTHER READING 48
INDEX 48

A HISTORY OF ALIEN CONTACT

Humanity has been troubled by the alien menace for many thousands of years. This guide looks at our experience with alien contact over the course of history, including a range of scenarios from UFO sightings to abductions, implants, and even attempted invasions.

To date, alien intervention has been largely ignored by the academic community and as such there has never been a comprehensive history of extraterrestrial activity on Earth. With our knowledge still fragmentary and large areas of study remaining unaddressed, the best we can do is to review some of the best-known incidents, those that dedicated experts and often amateurs have painstakingly researched for us.

ALIEN INTERVENTION HISTORIANS TEND TO DIVIDE THEIR SUBJECT INTO THREE MAIN SECTIONS THAT REVOLVE AROUND THE KEY EVENTS IN HUMAN/ALIEN RELATIONS – THE ROSWELL, NEW MEXICO, CRASH OF 1947. MAYBE IN TIME THESE SECTIONS WILL BE FURTHER SUB-DIVIDED – BUT REMEMBER THAT ALIEN HISTORY IS A NEW SUBJECT AND IT IS HOPED THAT FURTHER RESEARCH WILL ADD TO OUR KNOWLEDGE IN THE DECADES AHEAD.

▶ PRE-HISTORY (UP TO 1939)

This era covers mainly pre-Roswell events and includes hundreds of mostly poorly documented and fragmentary accounts of contact, abduction, and even attempted invasion right back to the dawn of man. Most of the case studies are reported only in part and some now feel more like legends and myths than verifiable history. However, these stories still have much to teach us. They prove that aliens have visited our planet for thousands of years if not more. And even these incomplete accounts suggest that the rate of intervention is increasing.

▶ MODERN (1939–80)

This period covers the spate of UFO appearances during and after World War Two, leading up to the Treaty of Greada in 1954, then up to the closure of the Dulce Airbase and the eviction of the Grays from the United States in 1980. These years represent a major shift in our relationship with aliens. After the Grays established a base on Earth under American sanction, it really did seem like Earth was "open for business." Unfortunately, the world isn't yet united enough to share knowledge of this encounter and the price of cooperation with the Grays is too high.

▶ POST-ROSWELL (1980 ONWARDS)

This era begins in the bloody aftermath of the Dulce Airbase battle and is characterized by an ongoing and covert war against several potential alien invaders. The Grays, the Little Green Men, and the Draconians all seem to be increasing their activity. But humanity is far from helpless and this period has seen the creation of the United Nations Office for Earth Defense in 2000 and major reforms in the Men in Black units.

Must separate fact from fiction... aliens real... Roswell real... Superman made up...

WE ARE NOT ALONE, WE HAVE NEVER BEEN ALONE!

THE PHARAOH ERASED FROM HISTORY

Any visitor to Egypt will quickly notice that in certain temples one particular cartouche has consistently been removed. Typically, it appears that some vandal has taken a chisel to the symbol and scarred the stone such that it's quite impossible to read the inscription. However, this isn't recent damage and radiocarbon dating has shown that most of the cartouches of the heretic Pharaoh Akhenaten were defaced shortly after his death in around 1330 BCE.

THE LEGEND OF AKHENATEN

Akhenaten was lost from history until discoveries in the 19th century gradually enabled archeologists and ancient historians to piece together his story. His great crime – and the one reason why his name was removed from history – was his attempt to transfer the religious allegiance of the priest class and peasants from their pantheon of gods to just one god, called Aten (or Ra).

What brought this story to the attention of alien invasion experts is the fact that, in the few pictures that remain, Akhenaten and his wife Nefertiti are represented as having elongated heads and long, thin arms – which implies that

they may have been human/alien clones. This evidence alone wouldn't be sufficient as images of rulers were often stylized in the ancient world, but further indications of an extraterrestrial link are offered by stone carvings that show the Pharaoh and his wife in "communion" with a bright light from the sky. Could it be that the Pharaoh is taking orders from a creature he believes to be Aten?

It's fortunate that a cache of diplomatic correspondence known as the Amarna Letters has been unearthed and we have gained valuable insight into what was happening during this period of Egyptian history. In one communication to the King of Babylon, Akhenaten writes: "We are overjoyed at news of the war against the Hittites. Great Aten has told me that we must grow our empire. He speaks to me in my mind and when I am taken inside his place of silver." 4/03 mh

The historical record about Akhenaten is frustratingly sparse but the evidence certainly points to an experiment in hybridization. Unusually, Akhenaten's body has never been found. Some believe that it was burned by an angry priest class after his death – an action unheard of in ancient Egypt as it would have prevented him moving on to the next world.

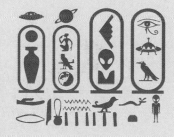

If the legend of Akhenaten was a conspiracy, possibly by the Grays, to use religion to control humanity, it backfired upon Akhenaten's death; riots swept Egypt and the old order of gods was quickly restored. The aliens would have learned that using religion to control humanity is a delicate matter.

A HISTORY OF ALIEN CONTACT

PRE-HISTORY (UP TO 1939)

Our understanding of alien intervention during this period is very limited, with the most up-to-date and well-documented accounts, not surprisingly, being the most recent ones. From the classical world, we rely largely on second-hand accounts and fragmentary texts, very few of which can be corroborated by other sources.

Perhaps the most famous biblical reference to an alien encounter is found in the Book of Ezekiel, which in its opening chapter provides a notably authentic description of the landing of an uncloaked alien pod ship.

"And I looked, and, behold, a whirlwind came out of the north, a great cloud, and a fire infolding itself, and a brightness was about it, and out of the midst thereof as the color of amber, out of the midst of the fire." As the text goes on to suggest there were alien reptiles that quickly shape-shifted into human form such that they had "the likeness of a man," this account would seem to describe the forced landing of a Draconian ship.

THE NEPHILIM

One area demanding more academic attention and research are the Gray hybrid experiments that were known as the Nephilim in ancient times and are best recorded in the ancient book of Enoch.

> NOW IT CAME ABOUT, WHEN MEN BEGAN TO MULTIPLY ON THE FACE OF THE LAND, AND DAUGHTERS WERE BORN TO THEM, THAT THE SONS OF GOD SAW THAT THE DAUGHTERS OF MEN WERE BEAUTIFUL; AND THEY TOOK WIVES FOR THEMSELVES, WHOMEVER THEY CHOSE. THEN THE LORD SAID, "MY SPIRIT SHALL NOT STRIVE WITH MAN FOREVER, BECAUSE HE ALSO IS FLESH; NEVERTHELESS HIS DAYS SHALL BE ONE HUNDRED AND TWENTY YEARS." THE NEPHILIM WERE ON THE EARTH IN THOSE DAYS, AND ALSO AFTERWARD, WHEN THE SONS OF GOD CAME IN TO THE DAUGHTERS OF MEN, AND THEY BORE CHILDREN TO THEM. THOSE WERE THE MIGHTY MEN WHO WERE OF OLD, MEN OF RENOWN.
>
> GENESIS 6:1-4

It's thought that the Nephilim were wiped out by the Great Flood. Could they have been a first, tentative step on the part of the Grays to solve their reproductive challenges by DNA engineering? Perhaps we'll never know, as even the information provided by the Grays is sparse about this chapter of their history.

THE HALF-LIZARD GREEK

Cecrops was a mythical king of the Greek city-state of Athens, most famous for two main things.

Firstly, he's frequently represented as being "a face with a tail." He was said to have been half-man, half-serpent, which immediately suggests a shape-shifting Draconian. Art historians have suggested that many of the images we have of him were created many centuries after his death and have most probably been idealized, as often happens with mythical figures. However, the contemporary evidence we have suggests a lizard-man in the top spot as one of the first kings of Athens.

Secondly, it's believed that Cecrops introduced a radical "breeding" program to high society in Athens by creating the concept of marriage among the promiscuous nobility.

Cecrops became a powerful ruler and left a dynasty in his wake that ruled for five generations. However, it's his intervention in the coupling of Athenian big-wigs that seems to have been his biggest legacy for subsequent generations.

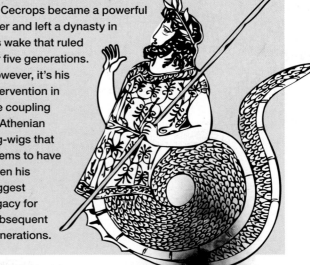

THE FOUR DRAGON KINGS

Historians of Chinese civilization have always taken the legend of the Dragon King as religious myth-tale but emerging evidence about Draconian designs on Earth has cast a different light on this segment of history. The fact that whole kingdoms were said to be ruled by "shape-shifting lizards" was enough to make even the most sceptical historian sit up and take note. There are also countless reams of imperial documentation from the era to back up the hundreds of pieces of artwork and pottery showing the Dragon Kings.

In classical Chinese mythology there are four Dragon Kings, each of which rules one of the Four Seas surrounding the Celestial Kingdom. In this interpretation Lake Baikal is included as the Sea of the North. These unusual kings are said to have ruled large tracts of land around 300–200 BCE and to have performed miracles such as flying and firing heat over vast distances – and, of course, changing shape.

We know little about these rulers other than what has been written about them in classic novels such as *Fengshen Bang* and *Journey to the West*, but they've been featured in Chinese folklore for hundreds if not thousands of years. The four kings – Ao Ch'in, Ao Jun, Ao Kuang and Ao Shun – are said to have ruled from the seas, extending their control over any coastal towns and villages. The Dragon Kings were guarded by their own soldiers and, according to legend, they lived in underwater "crystal palaces" that could fly. Needless to say, their power is thought to have been unrivaled by any other warlords.

A ROMAN ENCOUNTER

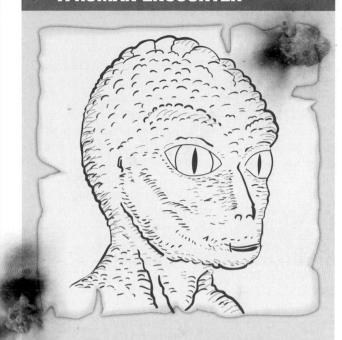

In 150 CE a Roman nobleman named Hermas, brother of Pope Pius, had an extraterrestrial experience on the road between Capua and Rome. His account was recorded in *The Vision of Hermas*, an early Christian work from which the following quote is taken.

"I saw a beast like a piece of pottery about 100 feet (30.5 meters) in size, multicolored on top and shooting fiery rays; it landed in a dust cloud. From a great pot walked a two-legged serpent, as tall as man most mighty. He was accompanied by a maiden clad in white. He spoke with her before she left the pot. The serpent saw me and, for a time, I was drawn to his gaze. I rushed forward and drew my dagger, ready to grapple with this demon made flesh while my servants fled in fear. Then, in the haze of midday, the great pot boiled away and vanished."

A recently discovered document, however, suggests that Hermas may not have been entirely truthful in his version of events. A slave who later became a free man gave a somewhat different account.

"Hermas ran faster than any of us servants. He even pushed one of the gray-haired water carriers over to aid his flight. He was howling and screaming like the wind and would not stop shouting "Big Snake!" until hours after the pot had vanished like the mist."

A HISTORY OF ALIEN CONTACT

THE MODERN ERA (1939–80)

Many experts believe that it was the use of the first jet propulsion aircraft and the exploding of the two nuclear bombs over Japan during World War Two that directly led to the massive increase in UFO sightings and abduction reports during the 1940s and 1950s. Indeed, it's no coincidence that this era also brought one of the classic science fiction movies and almost hysterical levels of panic about "little green men" or "invaders from Mars." Of course, there's some truth behind the science fiction, with aliens such as the Grays and what we now term the Little Green Men beginning to take humanity much more seriously, even seeing us a potential threat.

THE MODERN ERA IN THE HISTORY OF ALIENS ON EARTH IS DOMINATED BY THE EVENTS SURROUNDING THE ROSWELL CRASH. THIS INCIDENT EVENTUALLY LEADS TO HUMANITY'S FIRST FORMAL CONTACT WITH AN ALIEN RACE.

THE ROSWELL CRASH

No single alien event on Earth has generated so much debate, myth, and web chatter than the crash of a single Gray saucer in the New Mexico desert in 1947. It's important to note that this wasn't the first UFO crash on Earth but the timing couldn't have been more significant. America was in the grips of anti-communist paranoia, with enemies being seen behind every rock. Yet America was still essentially a free society with a powerful independent press, growing broadcast media, and some great pioneers in live journalism. It was into this fertile soil that a stray Gray saucer came down and was recovered by the US military. And, what's more, there were survivors on board.

▶ The crash of a Type 1 Gray saucer near Roswell is the most significant alien encounter of modern times, producing hundreds of witnesses and much photographic evidence. It received significant media coverage at the time before being clumsily covered up by the US government.

LITTLE GREEN MEN AND THE NAZIS

Exactly what did US Air Force pilot Colonel Benjamin R. Ryker shoot down during a raid over Germany in January 1945? Well, there are several amazing facts about the Colonel, who survived the war and went on to own a popular fast food chain in America. Firstly, he was a prominent member of 332nd Fighter Group, which is more popularly known as the "Tuskegee Airmen" – a group of African-American pilots who took to the skies over Europe from 1943 onwards, battling the Nazis and discrimination as they went. Secondly, and perhaps more importantly, he seems to be the only human pilot to have shot down a black triangle ship!

"We left the big birds to continue their flight home while I and a couple of other red tips [nickname for their North American P-51 Mustangs, which had unique red markings on the tail] broke off to fly over the nearby Warhearn Airbase, which we knew had been active. As I was completing my first pass, a black object flew past me at incredible speed. I banked right and lost eyeball contact with the target. I regained visual contact and noticed its

- ▶ The Gray saucer that came down contained a number of bodies and at least one alien that was still alive.
- ▶ In later contact with the Grays, we learned that the crash was most likely caused by a junior member of the crew flying the craft under the influence of an exotic substance known as "gleek," with apparently has a mild hallucinogenic effect on the delicate biology of the Grays.
- ▶ The alien survivors were taken to Groom Lake Airbase in Nevada. This later became a center of alien research and is known by the scientists who work there as Area 51 or "Dreamland" – the nickname arose because of the technological advances that were made there as they debriefed the captured Grays and examined the saucer.

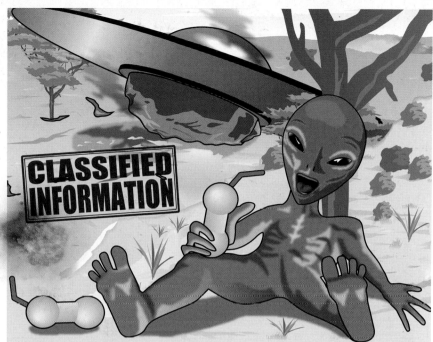

CLASSIFIED INFORMATION

Luftwaffe markings. For a few seconds I thought it was one of the foo fighters all the guys had been talking about.

"By now, I was alone over the base with a single anti-aircraft gun opening up. Their shots were so off target I suspected they were conscripted POWs missing on purpose, so I had a clear run. I flew a wide arc then came back in behind the black ship, which was now landing. It was a black triangle with markings on it. I'd never seen an aircraft like it but it was marked so it was game. I gave it a five-second blast of cannon and must have hit it because a plume of gray smoke shot into the air. With the heat off from any ground fire, I made another pass and saw the ship was now leaning to one side and seemed to be ablaze. I noticed a Nazi pilot dashing away but I didn't have enough ammunition for a second salvo. But what happened next took my breath away.

"First, I saw a small figure in a white suit climb out and run away from the wreck. It was wearing a much larger space helmet and can't have been more than a few feet tall. The next few seconds were something I'll never forget. The black triangle craft looked like it was just about to blow but instead there was a strange haze above it and then it disappeared into thin air. It's like the whole wreckage rose up and imploded."

FOO FIGHTERS

During World War Two there were reports from pilots on both sides about their planes being "buzzed" by fast-flying groups of lights or "foo fighters" as they were known at the time. Early German experiments with jet propulsion such as the Messerschmitt Me262 seemed to be particularly vulnerable to alien interest. It's now believed that these lights were automatic alien probes that had perhaps been alerted by the new speeds being achieved by these aircraft.

However, the craft Colonel Ryker destroyed on the runway was no probe. For starters, it appears to have been crewed by a German pilot and a small alien figure. Rumors of alien connections to the Nazis have persisted for many decades but for the most part with very little documentary or first-hand evidence.

EVIDENCE OF A PACT BETWEEN THE NAZIS AND THE LITTLE GREEN MEN IS HARD TO PIN DOWN. NO HYBRID ALIEN SHIPS WERE FOUND AFTER THE WAR AND IT SEEMS LIKELY THAT THE VISITORS HEADED FOR THE STARS AS THE NAZI REGIME BEGAN TO COLLAPSE.

A HISTORY OF ALIEN CONTACT

AREA 51 (DREAMLAND)

Groom Lake – more commonly known as Area 51 – is one of the world's centers of knowledge on all things extraterrestrial. It's attached to Edwards Air Force Base in Nevada. Area 51 covers some 80 square miles (207 sq km) of the most closely guarded space on Earth and for many years has been the home of the American response to the alien threat. The US Air Force still maintains a media blackout on the base many scientists refer to as "Dreamland" and most aerial images online have been doctored.

▶ MAP OF AREA 51

1. Perimeter extending some 10 miles (16 km) – exclusion zone and armed patrols.
2. "Dream Road" – slang for the main route through the base.
3. Alien compound (now thought to be unused).
4. Biodome, constructed in 1982 (appears on very few photographs).
5. S5 – alien intelligence and debriefing center.
6. S4 – part of the reverse-engineering block.
7. S3 – formerly a "Men in Black" building, now used by the UN.
8. Hangar 1 – known as the "Magic Box," this houses two crashed gray saucers, both Type 1s; the first is from Roswell, the origin of the other is unknown.
9. Hangar 2 – where alien technology is built into new human-made aircraft, such as the "stealth" designs that originated in the 1980s.
10. Bio-Science Block and ET morgue – a copy of the 1986 inventory logs seven Gray bodies in various conditions and two Little Green Men.
11. Data Block – a small complex of servers and systems analyzing alien data and technology.
12. S10 – a language block, where translations are completed.
13. The "Kill Zone" – where trespassers will be stopped, with the use of lethal force.
14. The "Gallery" – a huge concrete hangar used for testing of energy weapons.
15. Accommodation and guard blocks for those working on site – some 1,000 people.
16. The "UN Building" – a bomb-proof bunker facility so named because it's where the
    Treaty of Greada was signed.
17. The "Green House" – sealed containment facility where experiments are carried out on the virulent fungus known as Draconian Red Weed.
18. Geothermal power station provides the base with an independent energy source.
19. Blocks R1 to R3 are maximum security and are believed to be hospital wings for the various human/alien hybrids found after the battle of Dulce Airbase in 1980.
20. British Science Block – houses an on-site team of British scientists working on the crashed black triangle ship transferred from the UK in the early 1980s.
21. Auntie May's Alien Café – this military-owned diner is virtually unchanged from when it opened in the 1950s; it's the main social hub for the base and welcomes all species in an informal setting.

THE TREATY OF GREADA

This treaty signed by President Dwight Eisenhower in 1954 was the first formal agreement between humanity and an alien species. By the time the President met the Gray delegation for a face-to-face meeting, the Grays had been on Earth for a number of years and had already exchanged intelligence on other alien species as a demonstration of their goodwill towards humanity.

It's difficult now to ascertain whether the President felt coerced into an agreement with the Grays – clearly far more advanced than any life form on Earth – or decided that it was the best path to avoid interplanetary conflict. The essence of the treaty was to offer the Grays permission to abduct several thousand humans per Earth year, provided that the individuals were returned and they were unharmed by the process.

In addition, the Grays were allowed to establish their own research facilities at Dulce Airbase in New Mexico. The Grays were most interested in collecting human DNA but at the time their agenda wasn't fully understood. In exchange, the Grays agreed to provide intelligence on the various alien species that could threaten Earth as well as some of their technologies, including developments in stealth technology, the microprocessor, and the alloy titanium. Humans were also free to work on the crashed ship from Roswell and spent the next decades attempting to reverse-engineer it. Once the treaty was signed, most Grays moved to the underground bunker at Dulce Airbase although a couple remained at Area 51 as advisers.

> THE GRAYS WERE POLITE ENOUGH. THEY'RE KINDA FRAGILE-LOOKING AND CAN MAKE FOLKS FEEL UNCOMFORTABLE AS THEY SEEM TO BE ABLE TO READ MINDS. THEY CAN COME ACROSS AS A BIT VACANT BECAUSE THEY DON'T SAY MUCH. I SUPPOSE WE WERE AS STRANGE TO THEM. THEY FOUND US LARGE, CLUMSY, AND NOISY. I CAN'T SAY I EVER TRUSTED THEM, NONE OF SECURITY MEN DID.
> **SERGEANT OTTO RAINER, 422ND DIVISION, SPECIAL SECURITY OPERATION, DULCE AIRBASE, 1959–64**

THE BATTLE OF DULCE AIRBASE

By the 1970s abduction levels reached an all-time high despite the US Government's agreement with the Grays to contain the problem. It became quite obvious that the Grays weren't getting enough humans for their requirements through "official" channels, which restricted the volumes they could take. An FBI investigation noted a growing trend for abductees to be taken multiple times and, more disturbingly, there was an increase in the number of complete disappearances.

For their part, the Grays calmly dismissed accusations against them, suggesting that other alien races such as Little Green Men and Draconians were to blame. However, the US Government became increasingly suspicious about both the abduction numbers and the rumors of horrific experiments being done in secret at the Grays' complex in Dulce Airbase.

Finally, it was Jimmy Carter who in 1979 ordered that the agreement with the Grays be terminated. The US Government could no longer accept the status quo with the Grays, especially as military sources by now considered that the technological advances being handed over by the powerful and technologically sophisticated Grays in exchange were merely "trinkets" and of little benefit to humanity.

> **THE ENEMY WE ENGAGED AT THE BASE MAY BE DESCRIBED AS "ALIEN" IF THIS INVESTIGATION DECIDES TO USE SUCH A TERM. THE COMBATANTS WITNESSED WERE CERTAINLY HUMAN IN FORM, ALBEIT WITH RADICALLY ALTERED APPEARANCE, POSSIBLY ACHIEVED THROUGH PHYSICAL MANIPULATION.**
> **UNNAMED SOURCE, CLOSED SENATE COMMITTEE HEARING, 1982**

▶ DULCE AIRBASE

1 Known as "The Tube," this giant concrete cylinder was built to specifications given by the Grays and was used to store and launch Type 1 Gray saucers.

2 The Grays were working on a transit system using advanced laser-technology before the base closed.

3 The top floor contained a mixture of human and Gray security guards.

4 The laboratory level was opened to human audit on several occasions but contained no hint as to the horrific genetic experiments that were being carried out on the lower levels.

5 The alien housing level was sealed and had a specially created artificial atmosphere and gravity.

6 The lower levels were destroyed during the fighting in 1980 and, according to witnesses, were scenes of both carnage and some freakish mutations. Once cleared, these levels were sealed by the US Government.

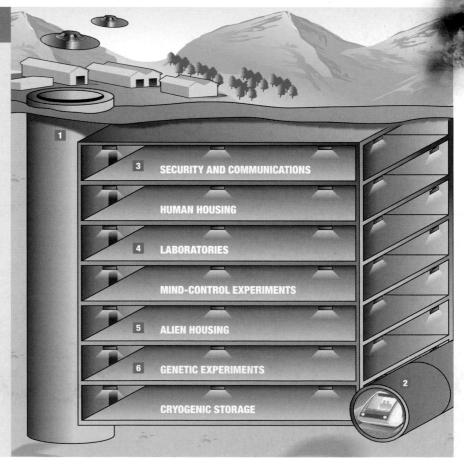

3 SECURITY AND COMMUNICATIONS

HUMAN HOUSING

4 LABORATORIES

MIND-CONTROL EXPERIMENTS

5 ALIEN HOUSING

6 GENETIC EXPERIMENTS

CRYOGENIC STORAGE

THE BATTLE

After it became clear that the Grays didn't intend to leave Dulce Airbase, President Jimmy Carter had little choice and removed them by force. What followed became known as the Battle of Dulce Airbase – a nightmarish fight for the Delta Force and the other special forces deployed. Witnesses to the battle spoke of flesh-burning laser guns, disappearing opponents, and – most frightening of all – many whispered of the hideous alien/human hybrid creatures they found on the lower levels.

EYEWITNESS ACCOUNT

One of the Army Rangers involved in the action in 1980 has agreed to provide a statement on the battle provided his identity is concealed, as much of the information around the incident is still classified.

"This was a fight like no other and believe me when I say this. I'd been in Vietnam years before and I'd seen plenty there but nothing like this. When my squad arrived, the entrance was abandoned. There were meant to be around 40 civilian scientists and security guards supporting the Grays in their work. We never found a trace of any of them – not even an item of clothing. There were typically 10–20 aliens on site at any one time but with the lack of initial contact we kinda thought they might have already bugged out. But then the shooting started. It was mostly our guys firing at every shadow and blur they saw. I didn't hear any return fire but the man to the right of me fell. As he lay on the concrete floor I could see there was a large part of his chest missing – no blood, it was clean as a whistle, like a chunk had just been vaporized. We fought our way down the levels, hardly seeing the enemy, just fleeting glimpses. They seemed to be using some sort of cloaking device but we soon realized we could spot them by making out their blurred outlines. My squad lost 14 men in that fight and it was hellish battling through those tiny corridors. We recovered four alien bodies in the end, don't know what happened to the others. But it was the creatures we found on the bottom level which I still have nightmares about.

CENSORED
WORDS DEEMED TOO SHOCKING FOR PUBLICATION

A BRITISH ROSWELL?

The UFO crash just outside RAF Woodbridge in Suffolk, England, in late December 1980 is the most well-known alien incident in the UK, with dozens of eyewitness statements over a period of about a week. Until this incident, the Ministry of Defense and the RAF had been open about "official" encounters with unidentified objects; for example, they released full transcripts of the so-called North Downs Landing near Wye in Kent in 1966. However, RAF Woodbridge was leased to the US Air Force at the time of the alien incident and there was never an official investigation into the alleged crash despite pressure from the British public. The only UK statement released was by the Chief of Defense Staff, Lord Peter Hill-Norton, who stated: "Whatever happened at this USAF base was necessarily of national security interest." This was a curious and cryptic phrase.

KEY EVENTS AT RENDLESHAM FOREST

▶ Throughout December 1980, there were reports from across the area of lights in the sky.

▶ The most controversial episode occurred on December 27. A member of the US Air Force went public in 1997 about what he witnessed that day, claiming that American forces fired missiles at and brought down "a dark, triangular-shaped vessel of unknown origin." Official sources stated that they didn't open fire on any airborne object and denied the existence of any ground-to-air missiles at the base.

▶ For December 28–30, the whole base was on lock-down, with local roads closed and flights diverted.

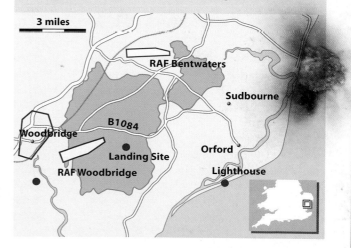

3 miles

RAF Bentwaters

Sudbourne

Woodbridge

B1084

Landing Site

Orford

RAF Woodbridge

Lighthouse

THE POST-ROSWELL ERA (1980 ONWARDS)

Since the collapse of the Treaty of Greada in 1980, humanity has been in a *de facto* "cold war" with the Grays. They and other species have continued to visit our planet and now, more than ever, we fear that it's only a matter of time before they come in force and to conquer. We have learned much from the Grays and a significant proportion of the information in this book has been sourced via Gray intelligence. But, as humans, we're more united than ever against the alien threat. Via the United Nations, countries exchange intelligence and cooperate far more.

We now know that aliens have been visiting Earth for tens of thousands of years; in fact, we have numerous documented accounts of their intervention in human affairs as far back at the Sumerian encounters around 3000 BCE. However, the key events of the post-Roswell era, as summarized in the timeline below, indicate the heightened threat we now face. The timeline presents an overview – there have been hundreds more encounters or crashes – by focusing on the main incidents that have sculpted our relationship with aliens and our current exposure to hostile invasion.

"It is clear to the members of this committee that our nation now faces a dual threat. Firstly, the forces of red communism surround us on every side, working in cloaked secrecy to bring about the destruction of our democratic tradition and institutions. Secondly, there are those unknown forces from beyond our world which we have discussed during this investigation and which can field military technology eons ahead of our own. In conclusion, whilst the first may be the most immediate and obvious threat, it is the second which most concerns us. We would strongly recommend moving to gain a United Nations Resolution on this issue as soon as is practical.

14/05
CP

Summary Report, Closed Senate Committee Hearing, November 1982, Volume 2, Pages 12–13, Presidential Summary

1980	1982	1983	1984	1985
A black triangle ship crashes near RAF Woodbridge and is recovered by the British and nearby American air force personnel. The Ministry of Defense covers up all evidence but a ship is recovered along with the bodies of three Little Green Men. The RAF Woodbridge incident is known as the "British Roswell." This incident led to the creation of the Ministry of Alien Defense to protect the UK; its first office is above Tiny Tim's tea shop in Canterbury.	A UFO flew over Soviet airspace and the nuclear missiles of the Byelokoroviche airbase in the Ukraine. Twenty R-12 missiles were programmed and targeted by the unknown triangular-shaped vessel and only prevented from launching by a last-minute intervention from a senior KGB official on site.	▆▆▆▆ For legal reasons, we would like to state that a cloaked Draconian vessel did not crash in Nigeria in 1983 and that three reptilian bodies were definitely not recovered and taken to Area 51.	A Chinese frigate recovered a hexagonal UFO that was found floating on the surface near the disputed Sakhalin Islands. There were no aliens aboard but the Chinese government was convinced that there was a Draconian plot to take over the People's Republic of China and instigated nationwide checks, finding over 100 cloned officials during the first six months of investigation.	United Nations Security Council Resolution 1013 was a secret international policy agreed at the height of the Cold War that, should an extraterrestrial biological entity survive a crash landing, the country holding that being would assume responsibility for its interrogation and extermination. Nations begin sharing information on aliens.

A HISTORY OF ALIEN CONTACT
UFO CONTACTS SINCE 1982

This is a global thing... must link up with groups around the world...

The startling graph on the right clearly shows an alarming increase in the frequency of alien intrusion into our airspace. It should be noted that these figures exclude any contacts outside Earth's atmosphere. In addition, it is currently impossible for our authorities to detect cloaked vessels such as Draconian pod ships. This data covers Confirmed Contacts supplied by reliable military and government sources – these aren't reports of people "seeing something in the sky."

THERE WERE OVER 70,000 UFO SIGHTINGS IN NORTH AMERICA ALONE IN 2010, WITH SIMILAR NUMBERS ACROSS CHINA AND THE RUSSIAN FEDERATION. THE IMPLICATIONS ARE CLEAR. THE ALIENS ARE GROWING MORE CONFIDENT OF THEIR SUPREMACY OVER EARTH AND ARE POSSIBLY MOVING INTO THE FINAL PHASES BEFORE A MAJOR MILITARY INTERVENTION ON OUR PLANET.

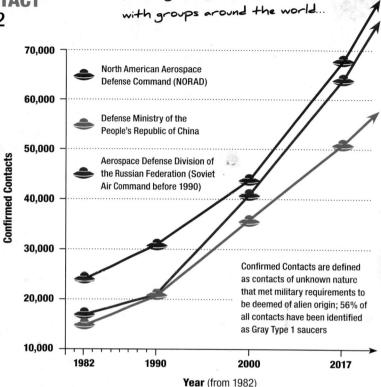

North American Aerospace Defense Command (NORAD)

Defense Ministry of the People's Republic of China

Aerospace Defense Division of the Russian Federation (Soviet Air Command before 1990)

Confirmed Contacts are defined as contacts of unknown nature that met military requirements to be deemed of alien origin; 56% of all contacts have been identified as Gray Type 1 saucers

Confirmed Contacts (y-axis): 10,000 – 70,000

Year (from 1982): 1982, 1990, 2000, 2017

1991

An Iranian diplomat in Iraq collapsed and started to "melt like wax." It was later discovered that he had no belly button and bore the telltale mark on the back of his neck indicating that he had been a clone. Unfortunately, his remains were destroyed during the first Gulf War.

1997

A student walked into the US embassy in Beijing claiming to have a message from the species we know as the Little Green Men. In poorly written English, the letter contained several very advanced mathematical concepts as evidence of authenticity. The note demanded the removal of all versions of the movie *Mars Attacks* and threatened the destruction of several cities if this instruction wasn't carried out.

2000

The United Nations Office for Earth Defense (UNED) was created as a separate entity from The United Nations Office for Outer Space Affairs. The new body was – and is – supported by the governments of all major nations and took over direct control of the worldwide network of "Men in Black" units. Part of the organization's brief is to gradually open the public's mind to the existence of extraterrestrial life.

2002

The United Nations Office for Earth Defense published its core document, "A Blueprint for the Defense of Earth," which includes the famous ET Invasion Matrix. It recommends that governments continue to deny the existence of extraterrestrial life.

2014

NASA lost contact with the Spirit rover on Mars. One grainy half-picture appears to show a tiny green figure urinating on the rover. NASA denied these claims, citing "excessive condensation in the circuits" as the reason for lost contact.

IT'S CLEAR THAT A FORCE FROM BEYOND OUR SOLAR SYSTEM IS CURRENTLY MONITORING OUR ACTIVITIES AND A SIMPLE EXTRAPOLATION OF THE STATISTICS INDICATES THAT THEIR PLANS ARE ESCALATING.

ALIEN CONTACT AND ABDUCTION

Although a surprise to a majority of the population, a full-scale alien invasion of this planet would in reality be the conclusion of hundreds if not thousands of encounters over the past few thousand years.

Perhaps alien races have always been watching Earth, keeping a cold, pupil-free eye on the development of the primitive species that live here. What we do know is that the "pre-invasion" – a term used by ET preppers – has already begun.

This includes covert actions by the sneaky Draconians to take over the planet by stealth and the testing of our defenses by the aggressive black triangle ships of the Little Green Men. The largest body of evidence, however, comes from the hundreds of thousands of UFO sightings and abduction cases that are being reported every year around the world.

ALIEN CONTACT

This is generally viewed as a positive experience in which a human is introduced for the first time to a life form from another world. The alien visitors will often go to great lengths to reduce fear or distress and the process is tightly managed from their perspective.

ALIEN ABDUCTION

This is the aggressive act of taking humanoids without their permission and against their will. It can involve painful experimentation, the implanting of alien tracking devices, or even cloning and DNA manipulation.

ALIEN ENCOUNTER LEVEL

FACE TO FACE WITH ET

Based on the work of astronomer and UFO researcher J. Allen Hynek, the Encounter Level was first suggested in his 1972 book *The UFO Experience: A Scientific Inquiry*. It has been developed and adopted by the United Nations Office for Earth Defense to provide a scale of alien contact and was most famously used in the Steven Spielberg movie *Close Encounters of the Third Kind*.

> **IF WE ARE GOING TO RESIST AN INVASION OF OUR PLANET THEN OUR FIRST LINE OF DEFENSE MUST BE KNOWLEDGE. THE ENEMY WILL NOT WILLINGLY REVEAL THEIR PLANS SO WE MUST RECORD, CALCULATE, AND ANALYZE, AS OUR VERY SURVIVAL MAY DEPEND UPON IT.**
> **ALBERT EINSTEIN, NEW YORK CITY**

ENCOUNTER LEVEL 1
FIRST KIND

▶ UFO sighted by a witness.
▶ Unexplained lights in the sky.
▶ Being buzzed by an unknown vessel.
▶ Witnesses hear strange noises or smells.
▶ It's estimated that around 62% of unconfirmed Level 1 sightings are either hoaxes or cases of mistaken identification.

ENCOUNTER LEVEL 2
SECOND KIND

▶ UFO makes a landing on Earth that may or may not be witnessed.
▶ Evidence of landing or burn marks.
▶ Possible effects on car engines.
▶ No alien beings are seen during a Level 2 encounter but they may be heard over radios.
▶ There were over 3,000 confirmed Level 2 encounters in the United States and Canada between 2010 and 2017.

ALIEN CONTACT AND ABDUCTION
DEALING WITH HOSTILE ALIENS?

In 2005 a level of hostility index was added to the scale to make clear the nature of the encounter – running from friendly contact established to a bad case of internal probing, extreme danger, and high likelihood of invasion.

In the early 1900s, when alien science was in its infancy, it was safely assumed that any contact with beings from other worlds would be friendly (level 2) or at worst unclear (level 3). The fiction of H.G. Wells and others was just for entertainment. But the increasing hostility of contact from the 1940s and the jet age onwards has convinced over 95% of qualified alien experts that we can expect an invasion encounter (level 4) within the next few decades.

1 FRIENDLY CONTACT ESTABLISHED
Some level of communication or possibly agreed next meeting. No obvious danger to humanity, potential for longer-term contact.

2 FIRST CONTACT ESTABLISHED
Both parties acknowledge each other but only limited contact made. Neither species threatened and no violence used.

3 UNCLEAR ALIEN INTENTION
Both parties acknowledge each other but no dialogue maintained. Alien attitude to humanity unclear.

4 AGGRESSIVE ALIEN CONTACT
Threatened with weapons. Alien forces make it clear that they have no wish to communicate. Humans may be abducted; could involve fatalities.

ENCOUNTER LEVEL 3
THIRD KIND

- ▶ Visible aliens, typically landed or manifested.
- ▶ Aliens may be disturbed at a landing site.
- ▶ Some form of contact – planned or unplanned.
- ▶ Many reports coming into the Ministry mistake known species for new ones – with witnesses creating features they have seen in fiction.

ENCOUNTER LEVEL 4
FOURTH KIND

- ▶ Abduction either against will or by agreement.
- ▶ Boarding of alien craft.
- ▶ Examination and possible implant of alien technology into humans.
- ▶ The great majority of Level 4 encounters are hostile, with abductions making up the biggest portion. Abductees may be held in a craft and taken into orbit.

ENCOUNTER LEVEL 5
FIFTH KIND

- ▶ Aliens arrive in significant numbers on Earth.
- ▶ Loss of life due to hostile action, which may be accidental.
- ▶ Evidence of invasion intent or open contact with humanity.
- ▶ Dubbed by ET preppers as "Alien Invasion Day" – it's possible that a Level 5 encounter could be peaceful.

ALIEN CONTACT AND ABDUCTION

FIRST-CONTACT PROTOCOLS

Since the breakdown of the American treaty with the Grays in 1979, it's safe to say that humanity has no official relationship with any alien species. Since its creation in 2000, the United Nations Office for Earth Defense and our various international Men in Black units have tried making contact with various species such as the Nordics, but to date none has shown any willingness to establish ongoing contact. Recently a paper from the United Nations Office for Earth Defense conjectured that Earth may have been included in some kind of "sphere of influence" whereby species such as the Grays or Draconians declare our solar system a no-go area for other aliens but as yet there isn't any real evidence to support this.

ARE ANY ALIENS FRIENDLY?

Throughout this guide, we have assumed that any alien visitors will be hostile. That's what all the evidence points to and that's what the experts currently think. However, we shouldn't close our minds to the possibility that we will encounter friendly aliens, those willing to help us and possibly even ally with us to defend the planet.

> **IF ALIENS VISIT US, THE OUTCOME WOULD BE MUCH AS WHEN COLUMBUS LANDED IN AMERICA, WHICH DIDN'T TURN OUT WELL FOR THE NATIVE AMERICANS.**
> **PROFESSOR STEPHEN HAWKING**

OFFICIAL FIRST-CONTACT PROTOCOLS

SAYING "HELLO" TO ET

The alien first-contact protocol is taken from the Ministry of Alien Defense operations manual and may be used where you encounter a species that appears to be friendly.

Preferably all first contact should go through the Ministry of Alien Defense or the United Nations Office for Earth Defense, but sometimes this isn't possible. These authorities have teams of highly trained first-contact specialists, but if you're up for trying first contact yourself then establishing a medium of communication is the first important step.

As a final word on the actual contact, be wary of misunderstandings. Aliens may not comprehend our emotions and if you're taken aboard a ship or subject to a physical examination, it may be better to just bear with it. There's such a thing as "voluntary abduction," where a human willingly goes with an alien species.

THE UNITED NATIONS HAS RECOGNIZED THAT PEACEFUL CONTACT WITH AN ALIEN INTELLIGENCE IS THE WORLD'S TOP PRIORITY AFTER SOLVING GLOBAL HUNGER AND THE ENVIRONMENTAL CRISIS. HUMANITY IS IN DESPERATE NEED OF AN ALIEN ALLY. ALTHOUGH MUCH OF THIS GUIDE IS ABOUT RESISTANCE, IF YOU GET THE CHANCE TO BUILD AN ALLIANCE WITH POWERFUL NEW FRIENDS, TAKE IT.

Type I Gray saucer – I think!

STEP 1
ASSESSMENT

Ascertain species and intent. Use the knowledge from this guide. Is the species one of those outlined in this book? Do you recognize the ship? If you can, take a position of cover and observe. Make no sudden movements and remain calm. If possible, avoid using a mobile phone as any signals may be misinterpreted.

Give up Italian evening class and find out where I can learn binary code

ALIEN CONTACT AND ABDUCTION
ALIEN COMMUNICATION

In communication, try Earth languages first – the aliens may have studied our planet and learned the language. The official phrase should be, "Welcome to Earth. This is the home of the humans. We talk in peace." We know it sounds strange but of the thousands of first-contact phrases this has been deemed the easiest to understand and translate. Don't be tempted to "mix it up" a bit or introduce any slang – you must work to reduce the scope for misunderstanding.

▶ Many aliens have telepathic abilities, so remember to open your mind and "listen" carefully for any messages. At first these messages in your head may be garbled and confused. Have patience and work slowly.

▶ If you find that you're unable to communicate with the visitors through language or telepathy, mathematics is your next option. Try drawing a simple shape on the ground – mark out, for example, an equilateral triangle – showing that all sides are equal. Or list a few prime numbers using dots. An advanced species will soon realize that you have some level of intelligence.

Remember that it's not just about the language – an alien may have mastered an Earth tongue but human concepts may still be a complete mystery to him. For example, Grays have no understanding of emotion as we feel it, while Nordics struggle to grasp our aptitude for creating war.

Radiation levels?

STEP 2
COMMUNICATION

Slowly approach the craft or the alien being, with your two hands out by your side and open, showing that you mean them no harm. This movement is designed to establish your "peaceful" intent. If they vaporize you with phasers, you know they're hostile. If you're concerned about residual radiation, ensure that you're wearing tinfoil underpants.

I don't trust their grabby hands

STEP 3
OUTCOME

Don't become frustrated if you're unable to establish communication – essentially first contact is all about both species making it clear that they aren't going to exterminate each other on sight. If you have a successful "silent contact," this will be something for you – as the technologically inferior species – to build upon.

ALIEN CONTACT AND ABDUCTION

ALIENS AND THE LAW

Let's be clear about this: Earth isn't a signatory to any intergalactic accords and has no agreements with alien species to help us govern the behavior of individual aliens on this planet. However, the Grays and Nordics have a principle known as "Universal Species Law" by which it's understood that no alien species has the right to be on our planet without authority unless they first makes themselves known to us. For the Draconians this is a moot point as they consider our planet to be their property anyway. But under our laws here on Earth, you're fully entitled to take on any alien being you discover acting against the good of humanity, subject to the normal constraints of the law. Here are a few legal pointers to get you started.

1 BE CERTAIN A CRIME IS HAPPENING

Don't try to make a citizen's alien arrest unless you see an actual crime taking place – just because aliens are here, it doesn't mean you should spring into action with a golf club or baseball bat. They may have come in peace but your actions could start a war that would finish off our planet

You must determine whether or not a crime is taking place. If, for example, you see a human being hauled away or witness a couple of Little Green Men mugging a small child to steal a lollipop, then by all means get ready to intervene with the full support of human and Universal Species Law.

2 THINK BEFORE YOU ACT

Think very hard before trying to make an arrest or restrain an alien being – a devious Draconian may change form and make it look like you've just attacked an old lady. Other aliens may be armed or be ready to resist. In some cases it may be best to wait for the Men in Black or other qualified humans. If you decide on action, be firm but try to avoid injury to the alien where possible.

3 DETAIN AND CALL FOR HELP

If you manage to restrain an alien being, even if the rest of its party fly off in their vessel, detain the creature and call for help. An alien prisoner is invaluable to the security forces here on Earth so don't be tempted to do any amateur probing yourself. Deadly force isn't permitted unless the alien is a physical threat to yourself or others. If the creature uses any "mind control" techniques you may use reasonable force to incapacitate its brain, normally with a big stick.

Call for help as soon as possible and, when the Men in Black arrive, ensure that you explain every detail you can. Use any witnesses you have to explain what happened. In the United States during the 1970s there were at least two military court hearings held in secret in which humans were accused by Grays of violent and unprovoked attacks, so don't be tempted to start applying any "human justice" to your prisoner.

THE FOLLOWING LEGAL EXPRESSION APPLIES TO ALL CITIZENS OF THE UNITED STATES:

The President of the United States requests and requires all those whom it may concern to allow the bearer to move freely without let or hindrance, and to afford the bearer such assistance and protection as may be necessary from other hostile alien life forms.

Any non-human life form should be aware that any harm to the aforementioned humanoid of Earth will result in the strictest sanction from humanity and the planet Earth, in accordance with Universal Species Law.

▶ REPORTING AN ALIEN CONTACT

Any UFO sighting, first contact or even abduction should be reported as soon as possible. Don't be alarmed if a unit of the Men in Black turns up and conducts a face-to face interview with you. In a first-contact scenario you'll almost certainly be invited for debriefing at one of the sites of the United Nations Office for Earth Defense; in the United States this will be a Ministry of Alien Defense site, where coffee and donuts are often provided.

ALIEN CONTACT FORM 333/22B		
Name Kevin Dwebble	**Number of witnesses** Just me	**Contact details** Ipswich, Massachusetts
Location My back yard	**Event duration** One uncomfortable night	**Time and date of event** 1.57am, 17th July
Level of encounter Too close	**Nature of aliens** Gray colored	**Friendly to hostile 1–10** 5 or 6
Alien species (if recognized) X-files aliens	**Sketch of species/numbers** *I call them "sky people"*	**Sketch of craft**
Number of aliens encountered 3 or 4 — it was dark!		
Number of craft/ships encountered One silver saucer		
Is this your first encounter with an alien life form? If "No," please give details.	No, I have seen this saucer before. I spotted it last year with my telescope and I've seen it hovering above my house before.	
Have you or a member of your family been abducted before? If "Yes," please give details.	I haven't been abducted but my Grandad said he was taken all the time by the "sky people." They put him in a loony bin but I knew he was telling the truth.	
Describe in your own words what happened. **Your account should be as complete as possible.**		

I was returning from a Star Trek special event at the multiplex (only $5 entry on Wednesday night) & I heard a deep hum. I went to my back yard and a saucer was hovering. I tried to make the Vulcan symbol for peace but must have got it wrong as next thing I knew I woke up in a cold, sterile silver room. I don't remember much else but I now have some discomfort in my neck and there is a slight bump at the back of it. I rang Grandad and he told me this was the work of the "sky people."

ALIEN CONTACT AND ABDUCTION

ALIEN ABDUCTIONS

This undeniable phenomenon continues to blight the lives of hundreds of thousands of people around the world. For example, an American government investigation in 1970 estimated that up to 100,000 people every year were being abducted, while figures from the People's Republic of China two decades later reveal that an estimated 175,000 people are reported to have been abducted by alien forces in northern China alone. Since the closure of Dulce Airbase in the United States and the current "cold war" with the Grays, things have only got worse.

Billions of dollars are being spent on covert operations to restrict these numbers but one alien research body has estimated that more than two million people are taken every year and the total could reach five million by 2030.

MORE AND MORE HUMANS ARE BEING TAKEN BY ALIEN FORCES AND, ACCORDING TO SOME SOURCES, A GROWING PERCENTAGE AREN'T BEING RETURNED. FOR COUNTLESS NATIONAL GOVERNMENTS AROUND THE WORLD, ALIEN ABDUCTIONS ARE FACT AND EVERY EFFORT IS NOW BEING MADE TO STEM THIS TIDE.

FACTS ABOUT ABDUCTIONS

▶ Around 80% of abductions are by Gray aliens and involve transportation to their saucers.
▶ Our best figures indicate that over 95% of abductees are returned and that over half of all abductions take place from the bedroom.
▶ Around 60% of those abducted are unaware that they've been taken, many only getting hints through flashbacks.
▶ If you've been abducted once, you're eight times more likely to be abducted again. Members of your family are similarly at increased risk of being taken.
▶ Abductions are rarely isolated events and spatial modelling has shown that they tend to cluster in specific geographic regions known to ET preppers as "hubs." Recently the Ministry of Alien Defense has noticed the emergence of "super-hubs," where hubs have expanded and begin to join up. Many see this as an important precursor to invasion.
▶ Alien abduction is a crime against humanity. It isn't the abductees' fault: they aren't alone as there are millions across the globe who've experienced the same thing.

ALIEN CONTACT AND ABDUCTION
HOW WOULD YOU REACT?

In the US the popular magazine *Health* broke the taboo around alien abductions by carrying out a survey, asking how people would behave if abducted. It provides a useful, if worrying, guide to the kind of resistance alien forces can expect from humanity.

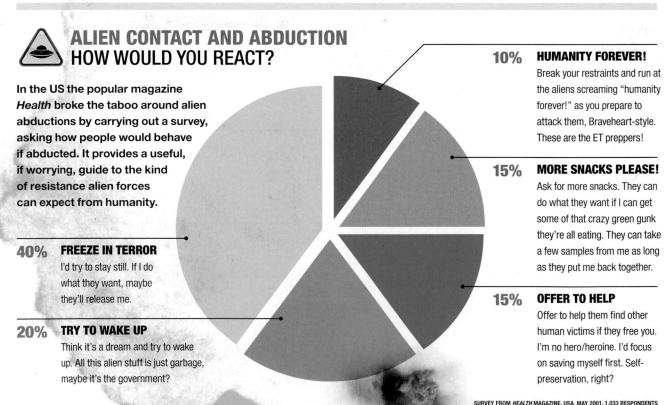

10% HUMANITY FOREVER!
Break your restraints and run at the aliens screaming "humanity forever!" as you prepare to attack them, Braveheart-style. These are the ET preppers!

15% MORE SNACKS PLEASE!
Ask for more snacks. They can do what they want if I can get some of that crazy green gunk they're all eating. They can take a few samples from me as long as they put me back together.

15% OFFER TO HELP
Offer to help them find other human victims if they free you. I'm no hero/heroine. I'd focus on saving myself first. Self-preservation, right?

40% FREEZE IN TERROR
I'd try to stay still. If I do what they want, maybe they'll release me.

20% TRY TO WAKE UP
Think it's a dream and try to wake up. All this alien stuff is just garbage, maybe it's the government?

SURVEY FROM *HEALTH* MAGAZINE, USA, MAY 2001, 1,033 RESPONDENTS

▶ WHO'S ABDUCTING HUMANS?

Numerous eyewitness accounts have enabled us to build up a good picture of exactly who's taking humans. In abduction science, figures before 1970 are generally considered unreliable as various "Men in Black" units during the 1950s and 1960s were routinely taking people they suspected of being abductees or alien clones, and in many cases these human abductions were mistaken for alien ones. Although such operations have now ceased, the image of these men dressed in black suits turning up to investigate strange phenomena has persisted in contemporary culture and fiction.

The Ministry of Alien Defense has conducted a major study into the identities of abductors and the results point the ET-like finger directly at the Grays. There's no doubt that other aliens are taking humans but in nothing like the same numbers.

My web forum says that the Draconian percentage is much higher — is the author a clone?

80%
GRAYS

Their prime reason is the collection of DNA and the tracking of various genetic experiments over time. It's for this reason that people are frequently abducted multiple times over their lifetimes. As in any experiment, the aliens are highly persistent in keeping their data set complete.

15%
DRACONIAN

Theirs is a subtle agenda that involves kidnapping people they see as important in the development of society. Often the victims are brainwashed and have no recollection of the abduction. This makes tracking numbers particularly difficult. In some cases they deem the abductee sufficiently important to be cloned and replaced by an alien-controlled copy.

3%
(UNKNOWN)

We shouldn't discount the concept that other alien races are both visiting our planet and abducting humans.

1%
LITTLE GREEN MEN

There have been a few cases of Little Green Men kidnapping humans but these have normally been associated with accidental encounters rather than planned operations.

1%
NORDICS

Although not technically abduction, the shimmering dimensional beings known as Nordics have in some cases taken those they deem of exceptional spiritual ability to other planes of existence.

WITH WEALTH AND POWER CONCENTRATED IN SO FEW HANDS, IT HAS BEEN ESTIMATED THAT THE DRACONIANS WOULD ONLY NEED TO CLONE AROUND 5,000 PROMINENT FIGURES AROUND THE WORLD TO EFFECTIVELY CONTROL EARTH.

ALIEN CONTACT AND ABDUCTION

EYEWITNESS ACCOUNTS

Still sceptical after all you've read? Well, close the windows and curtains, and prepare to read real-life accounts of some of the people who've been victims of the menace of alien abduction. These are all well-documented and proven case studies. If you're keen to read more, just search on any of the reliable alien abduction websites – you'll find thousands of similar accounts.

 SIGNS YOU'VE BEEN ABDUCTED

▶ You wake up in a completely different location, miles from your home with no recollection of how you got there.

▶ You experience unexplained periods of "lost time" that can sometimes amount to days. Normally you don't find yourself with an unexpected tan or a new tattoo after a real abduction.

▶ You feel panicky and extremely emotional before going to bed. You feel afraid but you don't know why.

▶ You display symptoms of Space Adaptation Syndrome (SAS) or space sickness, which affects over 50% of humans who travel in space – these include dizziness and poor balance.

▶ You have flashbacks during the day or nightmares in which you're being experimented upon by black-eyed aliens.

▶ You discover an unusual implant in your body that professional medics cannot explain. Alien implants are typically associated with regular abductees. You may also discover new or unusual scars, or even notice the odd body part going missing.

▶ Under hypnosis, you reveal incredible levels of detail about the interior of a Gray saucer or the aliens themselves.

YOU DEVELOP AN UNEXPLAINED PHOBIA OR AVERSION FOR ANYTHING SURGICAL OR CLINICAL. IN SOME CASES, ABDUCTEES CANNOT VISIT THE DENTIST OR DOCTOR. THEY COMPLAIN OF THE CLINICAL SMELL AND OF FEELING UNCOMFORTABLE IN THE STERILE WHITE CONDITIONS.

REPORT 778/333/KHH
ABDUCTION LEVEL 3
SYDNEY, AUSTRALIA

"I woke up staring into these deep black eyes. I tried to scream but my mouth didn't move. I soon found my whole body was paralyzed. There were more creatures around me and I could hear a dull mechanical drone in the background. I could hear them talking in my head. A dialogue was taking place. Images of beaches kept coming into my mind. They were just popping up there like a slideshow. Crude pictures of scenery in which something was always somehow wrong. One had a mountain with snow at the bottom but the peak covered with bright, blooming flowers.

I blacked out again. The next thing I remember was waking up by the roadside. I was still in my pyjamas. I later learned I was 50 miles (80.5 km) from my home and I'd been missing for three days. I still get flashbacks to that night and I have woken up outside since then but have no idea how I got there. The worst thing is not being able to fight back – you feel like such a victim."

REPORT 344/566/KPP
ABDUCTION LEVEL 5 (ABORTED)
HONG KONG, CHINA

The next thing I knew I woke up in a cold glutinous liquid. At first I panicked as I felt something down my throat. I pulled hard and yanked out a slimy cord. It was long and must have reached into my stomach or lungs. I gagged hard before pushing myself up and through a thin membrane-like cover. The gooey liquid surrounding me stung my eyes as I tried to wipe it away. As my vision cleared, I could see two pod-like beds on either side of the one I was on. In one was laid the blurry image of a massive dragon-like humanoid. The other had a reddish-pink human figure. I climbed out of the pod, pulling several cables from my body, and ran. I don't remember how I got out but I remember a ramp."

17/
sr

LEVELS OF ABDUCTION

The experience of thousands of abductees has allowed the development of a list to help gauge the severity of an alien abduction. We believe that well over 97% of all abductions fit into one or more of these categories.

1 AN ENCOUNTER
An unprepared human may be "buzzed" by a flying saucer, their car may be immobilized, their home probed and scanned. An encounter may be random or planned by the aliens. For the human, it's a frightening and mysterious event, perhaps with a dark portend for the future.

2 TAKEN ABOARD
Aliens will either enter the home or take a human from their location by force. Grays will often use mind control on the abductee and a tractor beam to lift the "body" into their saucer. Draconians will often kidnap their victims while they are shape-shifting and appear humanoid.

3 SURGICAL PROCEDURE
The key difference between a Level 2 and Level 3 abduction is that whereas an examination may be completed during Level 2, including some uncomfortable probing, Level 3 always involves a surgical procedure. This could range from the insertion of a cloning tube to the removal of skin or organ samples.

4 PROCEDURE INVOLVING AN IMPLANT
Importantly, an abduction is rated at Level 4 when the aliens discover something of interest in their subject. Before a human is returned, he or she is implanted with a device to facilitate recapture and further data collection.

5 DISAPPEARANCE OR CLONING
Statistically, very few abductees completely disappear. Those picked up by Grays are normally part of a larger data set that the aliens are keen to maintain. Draconian abductees have a higher chance of disappearing, particularly if they've been selected for cloning.

WE WILL LATER LEARN HOW TO TURN A ROOM INTO A SAFE ROOM, WHICH WILL SIGNIFICANTLY REDUCE THE CHANCES OF A SUCCESSFUL ABDUCTION. AS TERRIFYING AS IT ALL SOUNDS, BE AWARE THAT THERE ARE MEASURES YOU CAN TAKE TO DEFEND YOURSELF AGAINST AN ALIEN ABDUCTION.

REPORT 211/994/KLO
ABDUCTION LEVEL 4
LONDON, UK

The following statement was made to the Ministry of Alien Defense with the agreement that the name of the abductee would never be revealed. The target was a British-Pakistani with a rare genetic and blood disorder that the Grays will do anything to examine.

"The first time they took me I was 15 years old. I was in Pakistan walking around our village and must have just blacked out. When I woke up I was inside a metal room surrounded by creatures. That's all I can remember. Since then, they've come every few months. Always the same thing. I just wake up on board their ship. They take blood then try to feed me some kind of green gunk. In 1991 I moved to England to pursue my legal studies and I was sure they'd never find me but they did. In a busy city of millions of people, they still found me and took me. I was beginning to think there was no hope. Then I noticed a small lump on the side of my neck. I was worried it was cancer but when I had it removed it proved to be a tiny metal tablet. A lady from the Ministry of Alien Defense took it and, touch wood, I've not had a problem since."

It was obvious to the Ministry that the Grays took a zealous interest in this victim because of the rare genetic mutation he carries. The Grays are fascinated by our genetic diversity and the spontaneity of our genetic patterns. They were clearly tracking this man for decades until we removed the implant.

ALIEN CONTACT AND ABDUCTION

ALIEN IMPLANTS

When alien defense experts talk about "implants," they're referring to the devices extraterrestrials have hidden inside humans for at least 100 years. The earliest reported implant was discovered in 1885 by Dr Thomas Clark at Colney Hatch Lunatic Asylum in North London. We still have some notes from the original medical report.

"Patient 4433 collapsed last night with more seizures. The orderlies reported that he was once more ranting about gray monsters and being taken to "the flying castle." I completed my autopsy this morning, finding much as one would expect of a drunken vagabond of the lower classes. As light streamed through the mortuary window I noticed a tiny reflection from the cadaver as it lay face-down on the slab and for just an instant I thought I caught sight of a flickering red flame, emitting from the back of the neck. Upon investigation, I extracted the minutest little mechanical item – pill-like in size and with a tiny red light. It measured less than half an inch (1.27 cm) but did indeed seem to have workings or markings on it. I placed it in a metal dish and asked one of the orderlies to call for Dr Smith. However, he was destined never to view the object. No sooner had it been left in the air than it fizzled and dissolved as if it had been placed in acid."

Medical Notes of Dr Thomas Clark, Volume IV, May 1885

▶ TYPES OF ALIEN IMPLANT

GRAY OR DRACONIAN?

There are three main types of implant and it's believed that only the Grays and the Draconians currently operate them. Little is known of the nano-mechanics behind implants as most seem to "auto-destruct" when removed from their human host. Typically, they're found in people who've reported abductions, but not all abductees are implanted. To further complicate the picture, a number of people found to have implants had no recollection of abduction, their implants being found during routine medical examination or operations.

⚠ ADVICE ON REMOVAL

REMOVING AN IMPLANT IS NO GUARANTEE THAT THE ALIENS WILL NOT SIMPLY ABDUCT YOU AND RE-IMPLANT AN IMPROVED VERSION. IF YOU HAVE BEEN IMPLANTED WITH A DRACONIAN "SMILEY," IT IS LIKELY THAT YOU ARE ALREADY TARGETED BY THE ALIENS. SIMPLY REMOVING IT WILL NOT STOP THEM COMING BACK TO FIND YOU. THE BEST POLICY IS TO REMOVE IT AND THEN CHANGE YOUR IDENTITY AS YOU WILL BE ON A LIST SOMEWHERE AS A POTENTIAL POD-CLONING VICTIM.

STARFISH
ORIGIN Gray
PURPOSE DNA tracking/unknown
DESCRIPTION Star-like implant; will be found throughout the body.

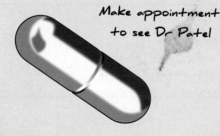

Make appointment to see Dr Patel

SILVER
ORIGIN Gray
PURPOSE DNA tracking
DESCRIPTION Pill-like implant; can be found at the base of the neck or behind the ear.

SMILEY
ORIGIN Draconian
PURPOSE Location tracking on Earth
DESCRIPTION A thin tab-like implant with "smiley" face motif; found at the base of the neck or spine.

HOW DO I KNOW I HAVE ONE?

The simple answer is that we don't currently have the technology to screen everyone for alien implants. Alien technologies have doubtless become more sophisticated and it's no coincidence that there are now more reports of "starfish" implants than the older pill-like "red," which was more common in the 1960s and 1970s. Further research is still required into the area of implants.

Some implantees have reported improvements in health and stamina after receiving their implants, while others have complained of listlessness and headaches. It has also been noted that implants tend to follow family patterns: one recent Russian study, for example, proved that a family had been implanted through four generations.

HOW DO I GET RID OF AN IMPLANT?

Firstly, you should never attempt self-surgery to remove a suspected alien implant. If you find the faint outline of a possible implant, consult a medical professional as soon as possible. Once your doctor has cleared you of any "natural" illnesses or claims "never to have seen anything like it before," the chances are you have an implant, particularly if you've experienced abduction or someone in your family has.

In the past decade the internet has become awash with budget providers offering low-priced implant-removal services, but the recent scandals around sites confirm that proper medical attention cannot be achieved on a budget.

If you're looking for a premium-quality implant-removal clinic, go for one that's approved by the Ministry of Alien Defense. One such clinic is Budapest Implant Solutions (BIS), which has operated in Hungary since 2009 and has become a center of excellence for implant removal. However, be warned that prices aren't cheap: an implant consultation costs around $1,000 and basic implant-removal fees start at $6,000; removal of a Draconian "Smiley" is listed at $10,000 plus. Discounts, however, are offered for families or repeat customers. Bizarrely, BIS sometimes offers Christmas or seasonal specials. A referral from your medical practitioner will be required.

NEVER ATTEMPT TO REMOVE AN IMPLANT YOURSELF. IT'S A SURGICAL PROCEDURE TO BE CARRIED OUT BY PROFESSIONALS, NOT A PARANOID LUNATIC WITH A KNIFE.

WHY THE IMPLANTS?

GRAY IMPLANTS

Gray intelligence tells us a little of their implant program, although current estimates suggest that hundreds of thousands of us have been "tagged" using implants. For the Grays, we're sure that implants are related to their DNA engineering work, allowing them to track human specimens either as control subjects or as part of some DNA manipulation program. In tests, implantees have shown no particular genetic defect, variation, or alteration, but of course this could simply be beyond our current level of science.

DRACONIAN IMPLANTS

The Draconian "Smiley" implant is by far the rarest one. Perhaps the most famous person to be host to one is Russian revolutionary leader Vladimir Lenin. It's said that his autopsy was meticulously carried out in 1924 as the party initially feared that he'd been murdered. The Smiley implant received scant attention, with the medical experts reporting it as a faint tattoo. Only later was it identified from grainy photographs as a Draconian implant. The fact that such an implant was found in a major world leader provides a clue as to the purpose of these devices. The Draconian agenda is all about taking control of the planet and current intelligence suggests that these implants are used to track prominent people who are possible targets for cloning.

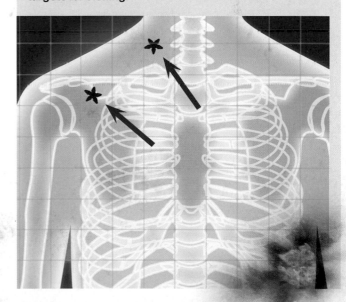

ALIEN CONTACT AND ABDUCTION

CATTLE MUTILATION

Humanity is not the only native species on Earth to receive the unwelcome attention of aliens. In the UK since 2004 an average of 5,000 animals per year have been reported as "mutilated" by the National Farmers Union. This figure excludes animals that have completely vanished in mysterious circumstances. In alien research this phenomenon is called cattle mutilation as over 90% of the animals taken are cattle, although the figures also include horses, sheep, and even dogs.

Cattle mutilation differs from any kind of predator kill in that the remains of the animal are typically found with surgical cuts, organs removed, and with very little evidence of blood. Investigations show this is clearly the work of skilful surgeons using laser scalpels, but as yet we have no agreed theory to explain this situation. Initial evidence suggests that cattle mutilation is a worldwide problem, meaning that hundreds of thousands of animals annually are being killed by alien interference.

The current hypothesis is that this is Gray activity and their prime purpose is to collect diverse biomatter from both the animals and the contents of their stomachs.

PROTECTING YOUR HERD

Farmer Geoffrey Parsons of Somerset, New Jersey, has spent many years working with the Ministry of Alien Defense after several of his own herd went missing in the long, hot summer of 2001. "Our little part of the world has proved to be quite a hot spot for alien activity. There's something about Central Jersey that attracts them. So, wherever you are in Central Jersey – do what you can to protect your own animals." If your herd is suffering from abduction, mutilation, or any other ET shenanigans, Geoffrey's nine-point plan can help – it has been proved to cut losses by up to 100%.

▶ Have you noticed any UFO, particularly saucers, near your farm in recent months? If you farm close to an airbase you're more likely to see these ships. Stay vigilant, keep your eyes on the skies, and learn to identify the different types of UFOs.

▶ Not every UFO is a threat to the herd. This rhyme is worth remembering: "If black triangle ships pass, they're free to munch grass; silver saucer overhead, better run for the shed." It's the silver saucers that go for the animals so keep a look-out for them.

▶ Ensure that all farm hands report any burn marks in fields. The aliens often check out farms before embarking on a program of animal abductions. Have them report any unusual noises or markings they find.

▶ Keep a close eye on how your cattle behave. Are they nervous or flighty for no reason? Does your dairy herd have a "vacant" or "distracted" look? Have they lost their sparkle or is their milk sour? These are sure signs that they've been buzzed by saucers.

▶ Always have a firm count of the number in your herd. Don't leave the animals for extended periods of time without a head count. If there has been an abduction or mutilation, the quicker you respond, the higher the chance that you can protect your animals.

> ONE THING IS CERTAIN – IF YOU LOSE AN ANIMAL, YOU CAN BE SURE THAT MORE WILL FOLLOW. FIRSTLY, DON'T BLAME YOURSELF. IF NASA CAN'T FIGURE IT OUT, WE FARMERS CAN ONLY DO OUR BEST TO DEFEND OUR HERDS. SECONDLY, AFTER THE FIRST ABDUCTION ENSURE THAT YOU CLEAN UP THE "CRIME SCENE" PROMPTLY TO AVOID THE OTHER COWS GETTING DISTRESSED. **GEOFFREY PARSONS, FARMER, SOMERSET, NJ**

Make tiny foil hat for pet gerbil Kevin, he is vulnerable at the moment

IF BLACK TRIANGLE SHIPS PASS, THEY'RE FREE TO MUNCH GRASS; SILVER SAUCER OVERHEAD, BETTER RUN FOR THE SHED.

- ▶ Prevention is still the best policy. The saucers use a beam to lift animals into the ship. A simple tinfoil hat on each cow can play havoc with this process – for whatever reason it seems to interrupt the procedure.

- ▶ After your first abduction, ensure that all cattle are safely in barns or yards after dark. Don't leave free grazers out in the fields. Create a protected area if you have to, by working with other local farmers – usually they will have experienced abductions as well. Draw up a rota and work together to defend the farms.

- ▶ Try to obtain comprehensive agricultural insurance that covers "stolen animals." No insurance company will pay out on abducted cattle but if animals disappear or are eaten by a predator then a good policy will cover you.

- ▶ Be prepared for the stress and worry of working a farm through a period of alien attention. Typically, ET will move on after a period of a few weeks without a successful mutilation but this period can be hard work for any farming family. Stick together and work with neighbors to defend the herd – don't suffer alone or in silence.

DOMESTIC PETS

MINISTRY OF ALIEN DEFENSE PET HOTLINE

According to the ASPCA, over 45,000 pets went missing from U.S. homes in 2017. Alien experts estimate that as many as 50% of them may have been kidnapped. Members of the public were so concerned about the threat of aliens to their beloved pets that a hotline was set up to support owners of domestic pets just as we at the Ministry of Alien Defense support organizations such as the National Farmers Union. However, we weren't prepared for the range of queries received, ranging from the worrying to the downright insane.

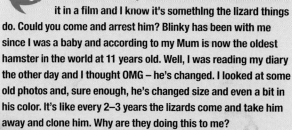

ANGRY HAMSTER OWNER OF DAYTONA

I'm worried that my hamster has been cloned. I saw it in a film and I know it's something the lizard things do. Could you come and arrest him? Blinky has been with me since I was a baby and according to my Mum is now the oldest hamster in the world at 11 years old. Well, I was reading my diary the other day and I thought OMG – he's changed. I looked at some old photos and, sure enough, he's changed size and even a bit in his color. It's like every 2–3 years the lizards come and take him away and clone him. Why are they doing this to me?

While it's true that the Draconians (lizardy-type aliens) do favor cloning, we have no documented examples of them cloning animals, let alone your pet hamster. Our guess is that you should ask your mother about Blinky's miraculous transformations and his unusual longevity.

MEDICATED OF TUCSON

Do the saucer people use animals to keep an eye on us? Last week I had the creepy feeling I was being followed but when I turned round it was just a pigeon. But, I don't know if it was me, but there was something "suspicious" about the way he looked at me. Then only yesterday, I was walking back from the pharmacy after picking up my prescription when I was "clocked" by two squirrels. I swear that they monitored me until I left the park. I think the aliens are using animals to observe us: is there anything you can do?

We have no evidence that aliens have used animals to monitor humanity. Their preferred method is via implants and cloning. In your letter, you infer that you're on some form of medication – if you ensure that you maintain the recommended dose you should find that the animals will return to normal.

BECOMING AN ET PREPPER

By this point, you may well be wondering "what's the point?" Haven't the aliens, with all their power, already won? Surely we may as well just enjoy the time left until our new extraterrestrial overlords arrive?

Only you can answer that question but read on if you're one of those who wants to open a can of triumph over any would-be invader, or if you want to make them wish they'd stayed in their shiny saucer, or if you want to kick ET butt all the way back to the Dagobah system. If this is your attitude, then you've got the raw material to become an "ET prepper."

An "ET prepper" – Extraterrestrial Intervention Survival Preparation Expert – is a person equipped with the knowledge, skills, and tools to defend himself or herself against any aggressive intervention by forces from beyond this world.

At many of the conferences and meetings about the human response to an alien invasion, much of the discussion is around how our armed forces should respond and the strategies open to us as a technologically inferior species. As a consequence, much of the thinking and work on ET prepping has been left to a growing community of amateur survivalists who now see an invasion by aliens as a major threat.

> THERE'S ONE GROUP THAT FORMS THE THIN BLUE LINE IN OUR DEFENSE AGAINST EXTRATERRESTRIAL INTERVENTION ON THIS PLANET. THEY ARE THE EYES AND EARS OF HUMANITY. YOU MIGHT CALL THEM "WEIRDOS." IN MILITARY PLANNING, WE CALL THEM HUMANITY'S FIFTH COLUMN. THEY'RE BETTER KNOWN AS THE ET PREPPERS.

MAJOR GENERAL BRANT, BRITISH ARMY INTELLIGENCE ATTACHÉ, NATO HEADQUARTERS, SPEECH TO THE DEFENSE COMMITTEE

PREPPING TODAY MAGAZINE SURVEY

A survey by *Prepping Today*, the best-selling survivalist magazine, indicated that the prepping community sees a hostile alien invasion as the second most likely cause of the apocalypse. This clearly means that those interested in surviving are beginning to take the alien invasion scenario very seriously indeed. In fact, according to a survivalist, alien defense items are its fastest growing segment with a year-on-year increase in sales of over 27% in 2017.

BECOMING AN ET PREPPER
THE GLOBAL APOCALYPSE

What do you think is the most likely cause of a global apocalypse?

This survey was completed at the 7th Annual World Preppers Convention in Portland, Oregon, and was compiled from interviews with 1,200 slightly paranoid ET preppers.

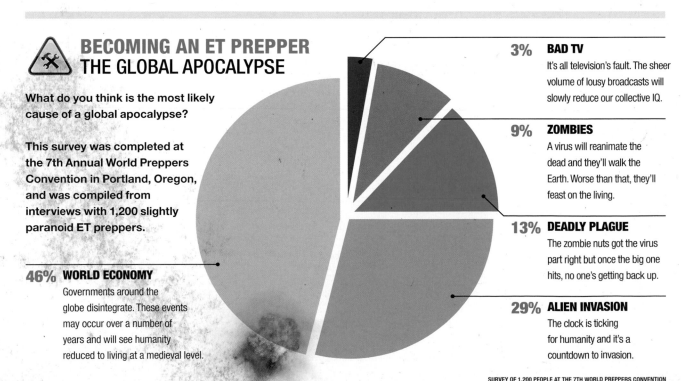

46% WORLD ECONOMY
Governments around the globe disintegrate. These events may occur over a number of years and will see humanity reduced to living at a medieval level.

3% BAD TV
It's all television's fault. The sheer volume of lousy broadcasts will slowly reduce our collective IQ.

9% ZOMBIES
A virus will reanimate the dead and they'll walk the Earth. Worse than that, they'll feast on the living.

13% DEADLY PLAGUE
The zombie nuts got the virus part right but once the big one hits, no one's getting back up.

29% ALIEN INVASION
The clock is ticking for humanity and it's a countdown to invasion.

SURVEY OF 1,200 PEOPLE AT THE 7TH WORLD PREPPERS CONVENTION

WHAT IS PREPPING?

ET prepping is not only about planning to survive an alien invasion but also a pledge to help your fellow humans in a fight-back against any would-be invaders. In 2007 an online group of ET preppers published what they refer to as their 'charter for the survival of humanity."

▶ KNOWLEDGE IS POWER

Get yourself educated on the threat we face: make sure you know your Draconian Smiley implant from your Little Green Men ray gun.

▶ PERSONAL PREPARATION

Apply that knowledge to defending your person, family, home, community, and planet against invaders from beyond our solar system.

▶ TRAINING AND VIGILANCE

Keep yourself fit, well-read, and updated with the latest information, always ready at a moment's notice to defend our species.

ALIEN WATCH GROUPS

Once you start talking to neighbors about the threats from outer space, you'll be surprised how many will share your concerns. If you're at all concerned about being regarded as 'the crazy neighbor' then why not invite a small group round, watch a decent alien invasion movie, then casually turn the discussion to how you would defend your street if there were to be an alien invasion. Serve some good food and nibbles to create a relaxing ambience. Any group can start informally, meeting perhaps once a week to review any unusual activity or UFO sightings. You may use content from this book as discussion topics for each session. You'll be surprised how quickly you can turn a formerly 'normal' street into a curtain-twitching, foil-hat-wearing group of ET preppers.

ET PREPPERS: CALL ME PREPARED, CALL ME CRAZY, BUT DON'T CALL ME PARANOID!

▶ PREPPING LOGBOOK

YOUR DAILY ET PREPPING LOGBOOK

One of the most powerful tools in every ET prepper's kit bag is their daily prepping logbook. In this journal you should record every action or activity completed each day. You can schedule tasks such as patrols or make notes on curious observations that may be worth further investigation. If time is short, start small and keep it brief. Think of each entry as something you're doing for the whole of humanity and keep motivated. At any meeting of ET preppers, all should share with each other items from their daily logs – this can be a useful way to join up any sightings or unexplained activity.

TUESDAY	
Saw Mrs Wright buying a significant quantity of meat – possibly reptilian shape-shifter?	Situation normal – she just has a new dog.
WEDNESDAY	
Investigated UFO sighting in nearby woods/possible abduction attempt.	Complete form of the Ministry of Alien Defense in New York. Leaflets to local homes.
THURSDAY	
ET preppers meeting – topic is black triangle ships.	Major headache following night out – possible alien mind probing?
FRIDAY	
Back bedroom is exposed to abductions.	Took the day off work/school and re-foiled the whole house. Local supermarket has now run out of foil. They call me the 'foil man."
SATURDAY	
Alien Invasion Tutorial reruns of Independence Day and Starship Troopers.	Copious notes taken and will test knowledge by writing an essay on Sunday.

BECOMING AN ET PREPPER

GETTING THE LOOK

Believe it or not, there are some members of the human race who aren't going to buy into the threat of alien invasion. Many are just happy to continue living their lives as if nothing is ever going to happen to our planet. Maybe they think it only happens to other planets and not ours? Maybe they dismiss the scientific evidence completely and just believe we can carry on regardless – oblivious to the fact that even now there are powers from beyond our solar system putting plans in place either to take our planet, make humanity slaves, or – even worse – wipe us out completely.

For the time being you're going to have to live in this world of "unbelievers." This can be a challenge for a hardcore ET prepper – after all, you don't want to end up sectioned in a lunatic asylum only to be left in a strait jacket when the invaders arrive.

This guy could blend into any office without arousing any suspicion

SIGNS THAT YOU'RE READY

1. You wake up every morning, look at the egg cartons and foil you've stuck all over your ceilings, and think to yourself – "today's the day."

2. You have boxes and boxes of aluminium foil stocked up at home and you add to them from various stores so that no one notices you stockpiling them in such large quantities.

3. You're constantly looking for ways to integrate aluminium foil into your wardrobe, maybe inside your school uniform or business suit.

4. You've become known as the "alien nut" at work or school but when taunted you just remain silent and cross the taunters off your "must rescue from alien tripod" list.

5. When looking up at a beautiful night sky, full of stars, you don't see anything but danger – you know they're out there.

6. When you catch a humming noise in the background, your first thought is that you're about to be abducted and so you race to your safe room.

7. You treat new people cautiously and frequently upset newcomers by accusing them of being alien clones.

8. Films like *Independence Day* and *Mars Attacks* aren't enjoyable movies for you – they're training videos to be studied and you take extensive notes.

9. Halloween is a bad time for you, so you just stay indoors – there are simply too many people dressed up and you don't want to make any more unpleasant mistakes.

10. You know the aliens are coming – for you it's not a question of "if" but "when," and it frustrates you that people take it for granted that we can live in safety on this gleaming blue planet.

THE EVERYDAY ET PREPPER

Whether you're working in the office, going to school, or just shopping at the local supermarket, the key to getting the everyday look is to combine safety and technology with an inconspicuous appearance and a nod to high fashion.

▶ A jaunty hat or beret will make you one of the "cool kids" but no one will ever suspect that it's lined with foil, thereby offering some protection against any alien mind probe.

▶ Dark sunglasses: no one said being an ET prepper couldn't be cool – they might have thought it but they wouldn't say it.

▶ They look like normal pants from the outside but on the inside they have a stitched lining of metallic foil fabric to resist any alien scanners. Man-made fibres are best, so you may want to consider purchasing a stylish polyester shellsuit to get a coordinated look.

▶ The pockets on these special pants, male and female, are extra deep, with space for both caffeine and travel-sickness pills in case you get abducted.

▶ An anorak is best in black as some aliens find it more difficult to see darker shades of color. There should be a pouch for travel pills in case you become ill during abduction.

▶ A built-in notepad is useful to record any suspicious events, ship sightings, or alien encounters. You may wish to design a discrete "utility belt" in which to store the various anti-alien items you want to carry. Find space for rubber gloves as you never know when you may need to take an alien sample.

▶ The male's standard sports coat or school blazer certainly looks the business but inside there are several hidden pockets for a built-in Geiger counter, special sunglasses, and a blood-testing kit – in case you need to screen for clones.

▶ The whole ensemble is made using the latest synthetic fabrics and polyester with proven protective properties against alien scans and their heat vision.

▶ The best footwear is a pair of blackened plastic running shoes, which look like fancy work shoes. You need to be able to move quickly should an incident develop.

▶ The male's brief case or school "bug-out bag" looks normal enough but contains 24 hours' worth of supplies in the event of an alien invasion while you're away from home.

REGARDLESS OF WHAT YOU'RE DOING, FEW OTHERS SHOULD SUSPECT THAT YOU'RE PRIMED AND READY TO SPRING INTO ACTION AT A MOMENT'S NOTICE.

BECOMING AN ET PREPPER

HOMEMADE PROTECTION

Several alien species make use of mind-probe techniques to give them an edge against a human opponent. Apparently our brains are so complex and confused – by intergalactic standards – that as a species we're particularly susceptible to mind invasions. Some aliens, such as the Grays, have a natural ability to "read thoughts," while others, such as the Draconians, rely on sophisticated equipment.

It has been shown that both species can read minds within a distance of 328 feet (100 meters), which means that you could be wandering down the street totally unaware that an alien is quietly picking your anti-abduction defense plans. Worse still, we can confirm that aliens can also implant "ideas" into your brain. So, if you ever find yourself clearing a saucer landing zone in your yard and wonder what you're doing – the chances are that you've had an idea implanted.

THERE ARE MANY TOOLS AND TECHNIQUES YOU CAN USE TO PROTECT YOUR GRAY MATTER – FOIL, MUSIC, SUNGLASSES. LEARN THEM AND NEVER LET YOUR GUARD DOWN. IF YOU SEE SOMEONE LOOKING AT YOU STRANGELY, JUST SMILE AND PULL THAT FOIL HAT DOWN A LITTLE LOWER.

HOW TO MAKE AN ANTI-MIND-PROBE HAT

Humanity's defense against mind-probe techniques is typically low-tech and comes in the form of our remarkable ally – aluminium foil. A simple foil covering cannot guarantee that you won't be probed but it does ensure that you're as resistant as you can be. In Ministry of Alien Defense assessments, a foil covering of at least 0.024 inches (0.6mm) thickness was found to reduce susceptibility by over 84%, while use of heavy-duty foil of at least 0.035 inches (0.9mm) will offer even greater protection.

The advantages of wearing a foil covering over the head, particularly when you're out and about, are obvious in terms of protecting your plans and schemes to resist an alien invasion. Even when an invasion has begun, it's worthwhile keeping your thoughts secret from those trying to take our planet from us. Luckily, with the reemergence of hats as a fashion item, you need no longer be considered "weird" as you can easily disguise your foil covering.

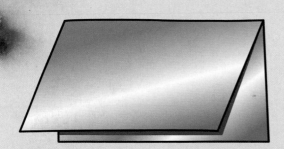

STEP 1

Fold the piece of foil in half, so you have a rectangular section with the long folded edge at the top. Use a smaller sheet to create a child's version. If you have a very large head, you may need to use two sheets taped together.

STEP 2

Fold the two corners as in the diagram so that the edges meet to form two triangles. Ensure that the shiny side is facing outwards as this has been shown to give a slightly improved level of protection.

MINISTRY OF ALIEN DEFENSE

BECOMING AN ET PREPPER
ONCE THE INVASION BEGINS!

Once the invasion has begun, you can put away any pretenses of normality – when cities are burning and tripods are marching through our streets you won't need to convince any unbeliever. Some of the more subtle tools of the hidden alien war can be discarded once a military invasion of Earth actually begins – for example, you'll be able to ditch the fancy pants or foil-lined skirt in favor of something more practical.

Remember, you may be travelling long distances on foot and sleeping rough as well as battling an unearthly opponent. Items such as foil-lined berets will become standard issue although they'll only provide limited protection against a sustained alien mind probe. The best advice is to go to an army surplus store and stock up to build a real "post-apoc" wardrobe.

STEP 3

Fold up the bottom edge of the foil so that it meets the bottom edge of the two triangles. You may wish to tape down the sides.

STEP 4

Fold up the bottom foil edge again, with the fold line running along the bottom edge of the triangle, and cut off any parts that stick out.

STEP 5

To convert this basic model into a foil "innard," simply fold down the pinnacle of the triangle (never cut it). Tape it down along with the folded sections. You can then mold the foil into any hat style, such as a Bohemian beret, a businesslike bowler, or a gangsta-style baseball cap.

> ⚠ **WARNING**
>
> **ALWAYS ENSURE THAT YOUR MIND-PROBE DEFENSE IS WORN CORRECTLY. AVOID THE TENDENCY OF SOME TO WEAR THE HAT AT A JAUNTY ANGLE – YOU MUST PROTECT THE WHOLE TOP HALF OF YOUR HEAD. IT CAN TAKE TIME TO GET USED TO WEARING A HAT ON ALL OCCASIONS SO IT'S WORTH HAVING A RANGE OF OPTIONS SO YOU CAN ADAPT TO FASHION AND AS THE SITUATION DEMANDS.**

Ask at Playgroup about different hat construction techniques

BECOMING AN ET PREPPER

PREPPING FOR FAMILIES —

The best ET preppers are those who share their hobby and passion with their family. Obviously your starting point is to ensure that your partner and any children are aware of the risks out there in space. You may want to use some of the material in this guide to create fun games such as "hunt the Gray" or "let's see if we can find a Draconian clone at the shopping center." Be creative with children and sceptical partners. At first they may not understand your fixation with watching the skies, but before too long you'll have them all sleeping in foil hats and doing the kinds of things that are going to ensure that our planet can survive an alien invasion.

RAF PREPPING

In the UK, the Royal Air Force (RAF) took overall responsibility for alien defense for many years, with much of the organizational material focusing on the threat from Mars. The RAF produced a series of leaflets throughout the 1940s and 1950s, including cartoon-type educational stories aimed at the young. This cartoon was published in October 1960 as part of the last such document, a 20-page leaflet curiously entitled *Communists Under The Bed, Martians Overhead*. At the time it fed into the hysteria over agents from the USSR and the paranoia about aliens from the "Red Planet."

COMMUNISTS UNDER THE BED, MARTIANS OVERHEAD

Published by MOD Publications
RAF 1957/7/33A SE7

BECOMING AN ET PREPPER
COPING WITH DISABILITIES

A recent poll of readers of *Prepping Today* magazine showed that 35% of subscribers described themselves as having some form of physical disability. It's clear, therefore, that disabled preppers are going to play a significant role in any human fight-back in an alien invasion. A war against invaders from beyond our solar system will be a war against the whole of humanity – everyone will be a target for them.

> ❝ THE ALIENS WON'T CARE IF YOU'RE DISABLED OR IN A WHEELCHAIR SO IT'S DOWN TO YOU TO PREPARE YOURSELF TO SURVIVE THEM AND MAKE SURE YOU CAN DO YOUR BIT TO SAVE THE PLANET AND HUMANITY. ❞
> **SHIRLEY "JACK-KNIFE" COLLINS**
> **PRESIDENT OF THE COLORADO PARA-PREPPERS GROUP**

Do not rely on electric wheelchairs, the aliens can control them

PLAN AHEAD

As a general rule, ensure that you have sufficient food supplies for at least 120 days. Stock up on any medical requirements and, if possible, develop a local network of supporting preppers. Looking ahead to a war against the aliens on Earth, think about the skills you can develop that would help humanity – perhaps you could adapt your house such that it could easily become a forward aid station, treating ray-gun burns, etc. Perhaps you could develop your skills in water filtration and supply our front line units with clean water. Not everyone will be out there firing rocket-propelled grenades at flying saucers but that doesn't mean you can't play a vital role – particularly in ensuring that any human resistance is well-supported. If you really want to invest in safeguarding our planet, consider creating a fully equipped base under your home – complete with communications and maps of your area.

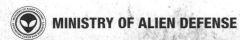

▶ BILLY AND THE MARTIAN INVASION

Billy is at home ill. He can't believe he's missing the baseball game, all because of this stinking cold!

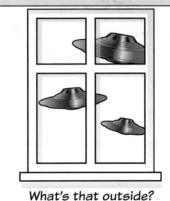

What's that outside?

Looks like flying saucers! From his window Billy sees that these Martians certainly DON'T come in peace.

The Martians defeat everything we can throw at them. Is this the end of the U.S.?

Then Billy remembers reading his science fiction comics... he has an idea and it's a real peach!

What's this? Is Billy betraying the country?

Billy talks the Martians through his homework. They think they're top secrets!

But all the time he's breathing his germs!!!

Some of the Martians aren't feeling so clever!!!

Meanwhile Billy escapes using an alien jet pack.

The Martians are ill, and soon start running!

The answer was in my sci-fi comics. I knew we could rely on our old friends – the germs!

BECOMING AN ET PREPPER

ET PREPPER PRODUCTS

The Ministry of Alien Defense regulates the many "anti-alien" products that have surged on to the market since people stopped watching *The X-Files*. Some of these products are decidedly dodgy, but by working with various trading standards organizations around the U.S. since 2004, MAD has been able to remove from sale over 100 rogue products – everything from anti-clone chewing gum to an Insectoid binary-language phrase book. However, this work has proved to be a drop in the ocean as thousands of new items are flooding on to the internet market – a recent example is a farcical leaflet on interdimensional Nordic Wisdom and how to get ahead in the real estate market.

Be warned, there are some useful accessories out there to help you defend your home, family, and planet against the aliens, but also watch out for useless products that could cost you dearly when you come to use them in action. Here are a few examples of some of the most popular pieces of garbage out there on the internet.

▶ CHEESY GLASSES

What if you could help save mankind and look cool at the same time? Well, that's exactly what you can do with these new NASA-inspired shades. Using the latest hyper-glass technology, these cool sunglasses protect your eyes from the glare of the sun but at the same time allow you to see right through any Draconian shape-shifting. Regular Earth humans will appear normal but when you chance on a reptilian invader, trying to work its way into a position of power, you'll be able to see its lizard skin – and then you can warn your fellow humans. But with great power comes great responsibility, so use your knowledge carefully or you could end up on the Draconian menu!

"SEE THE REPTILIAN SHAPE-SHIFTERS BEFORE THEY SEE YOU!"

PRODUCT REVIEW 👍👍👍👍👍

OK, so these sunglasses do look pretty cool but they fail on every other count. They provide no UV protection for your eyes. We have no idea why they're NASA-inspired and, most importantly, they don't reveal shape-shifters. All round a fashionable but misleading product, although the snake-skin effect is pleasing.

▶ ESCAPE-FROM-EARTH TICKETS

AURORA BOARDING PASS

FLIGHT NUMBER	REPORTING TIME	BOARDING NUMBER

"PURCHASE A SECOND TICKET AND GET A FREE WINDOW-SEAT UPGRADE SO YOU SEE EVERY LAST RAY-GUN STRIKE!"

Are you constantly worrying about an alien invasion? Do you like the thrill of visiting new places? Well, Escape From Earth may have the answer for you. Why not sit back and enjoy a guaranteed escape from Earth if we're invaded? Once safely aboard our third-generation super space shuttle *Aurora*, you can just sit back in your extra-wide leather seats and enjoy the fireworks. $200 per month per person doesn't just buy you peace of mind – it buys you and your family a fresh start on a new world.

PRODUCT REVIEW 👍👍👍👍👍

The subscription payments go through a Swiss bank account and all we can say for certain is that some rather unimpressive tickets do arrive if you start a subscription. This offer is an old-style scam. If you sign up to abandon your fellow humans in their time of need then you deserve to be fleeced every month!

ALIEN ABDUCTION INSURANCE

BMU* (Interstellar) Insurance

Cover: Full Time and Dimension

Name . . . .   Address . . . .

. . . .

D.O.B . . . .   Insurance No. . . . .

BMU (Interstellar) Insurance is the trading name of Beam Me Up Insurance Services Groom Lake Road, Nevada, KXTA	The company will pay the claimant £1 per year until their death or for 1 million years, whichever comes first.

Check out our policies for alien pregnancy, alien examinations and death caused by aliens

If you're being taken regularly into outer space by aliens against your will, then you're sure to be feeling the pinch in your budget. Unexplained days off work, stolen pyjamas, missing chunks of time, and the constant travel fares returning from wherever they leave you – it all adds up and could impose extra strain at an already stressful time. Help is at hand: the insurance industry has put together a "total care" package. Just because you've been abducted, it doesn't mean your finances have to be!

BENEFITS INCLUDE:

▶ A guarantee payment for every 24-hour period spent in the alien ship.

▶ A daily travel allowance for when you turn up unexplained hundreds of miles from your home.

▶ A lump sum payment for any loss of limb or if you come back impregnated by an alien hybrid.

▶ Access to a 24-hour abduction support helpline for claims, manned by people who won't think you're crazy.

▶ A professional and discrete device-removal service, should a medical examination reveal that you have an alien implant.

"BUY ALIEN ABDUCTION INSURANCE NOW AND GET A FREE 'PSTCHOLOGICAL THERAPY' PACKAGE, WHICH WILL COVER ANY THERAPY AS A RESULT OF A TRAUMATIC INVESTIGATION!"

PRODUCT REVIEW

As ever, the devil is in the details. The very tightly written terms and conditions of this insurance policy mean that short of an actual alien saucer landing and dropping you off in front of several witnesses, it's almost impossible to succeed with a claim. You're better off spending your money on hundreds of rolls of foil.

ANTI-ALIEN FOIL

Anti-alien foil is the only foil approved by both the United Nations Organization for Earth Defense and the Ministry of Alien Defense. In fact, with over 200 square feet (18.5 sq meters) of aluminium and titanium foil in each pack, you'll be able to protect your entire house against any unwelcome alien intrusion.

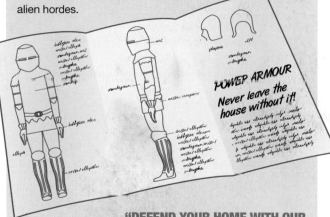

PROTECT'O'FOIL — Number 1 fashion accessory for conspiracy theorists around the world

ANTI-SCANNING FOIL

The special properties of aluminum foil that shield the brain from being read. Also works nicely as a rain hat that gives the "tin roof" effect.

But that's not all. With every box of ten anti-alien foils purchased, you'll receive our free guide to making foil clothes. Inside *Alien Invasion Fashion Police*, a 25-page booklet, you'll find everything you need to know about creating anti-alien foil "power armor" that you can wear while battling the alien hordes.

POWER ARMOUR Never leave the house without it!

"DEFEND YOUR HOME WITH OUR UNIQUE FOIL AND CREATE AN OUTFIT THAT WILL EVEN HAVE THE ALIENS DOING DOUBLE TAKES!"

PRODUCT REVIEW

Expensive, useless, and little better than what you buy in any supermarket, this product is nothing but a money-making hoax. Neither of the organizations mentioned has sanctioned this product, which seems to be little more than particularly thin foil in a fancy box.

BECOMING AN ET PREPPER

HOME DEFENSE

If you're serious about ET prepping, then you're going to have to make some major changes to your home as well as your lifestyle. The first few days of an alien invasion are likely to be confused times, with crowds panicking and various military units trying in vain to fight back.

You may decide to hook up immediately with a militia group or head off to help other survivors; whatever your decision, a strong, fortified home base is vital. For starters, with a few careful improvements you can drastically reduce the chances of any abduction or other pre-invasion alien intervention, and, when the fighting starts, you'll be well-equipped to support the war effort and help guide human forces to victory.

BUDGETARY CONSIDERATIONS

If you've already been abducted or have a healthy fear of the phenomena that affect millions around the world, then you may be tempted to start spending whatever is necessary to "secure your home" from the alien menace. But be wary: there are unscrupulous providers out there ready to help you spend your money on highly visual but largely ineffective and expensive adaptions to your home.

Take control of your finances by carefully budgeting income and expenditure. Earmark an amount for alien defense activity then stick to it. ▌▌▌▌▌▌

31/12 cs

AN INSIGHT INTO ALIEN TECHNOLOGIES

UNDERSTANDING THE TECH
When the average home owner thinks of home invasion, they consider high-security locks, double glazing, and burglar alarms. While it's true that some of these can help prevent an alien from breaking into your home, it's essential that ET preppers have an understanding of the science we're up against.

> **❝ EVERY ET PREPPER MUST GET TO GRIPS WITH WHAT WE KNOW ABOUT ALIEN TECHNOLOGY IF THEY'RE TO UNDERSTAND THE THREAT WE FACE AND DEFEND THEIR HOME AND THEIR PERSON. WE START OUR WEEKLY GROUP MEETINGS WITH A TECHNICAL BRIEFING: LAST WEEK IT WAS LASERS, THIS WEEK IT'S TRACTOR BEAM RESEARCH. ET IS HUNDREDS OF YEARS AHEAD OF US AND WE HAVE A LOT OF CATCHING UP TO DO! ❞**
> **SHIRLEY COLLINS, ET PREPPER**

THREAT 1
SURVEILLANCE
Every alien species known to us makes use of surveillance devices far beyond our current level of scientific understanding. For example, we know that both Gray saucers and Little Green Men black triangle ships can hover high above locations and obtain a full read-out of who's within buildings, their location and more. We know that a layer of lead (at least .2 inches or 5mm thick) significantly reduces the surveillance ability of the aliens. Lead has proven to be a highly effective precaution.

THREAT 2
TRACTOR BEAMS
Many of the observations around the alien use of surveillance techniques are equally relevant to dematerialization or tractor beams. To clarify, the process of dematerialization involves the human victim completely disappearing and then reappearing outside his or her home. The way this happens is by means of tractor beams, which lock on to victims and bring them up into the alien ship. We have examples of beams lifting people out of rooms in buildings, usually through windows.

BECOMING AN ET PREPPER
SELECTING THE RIGHT HOME

Although no steps can guarantee safety from abductions or provide you with that perfect location from which to lead a fight-back against alien invaders, there are a few simple rules that can help.

1 LIVING NEAR POWER LINES

It has been statistically proven that abduction levels are lower where a house is close to or surrounded by power or telephone cables. It's believed that any electrical interference can disrupt the alien teleportation system, meaning that the ship is forced to make a landing and complete a manual extraction – which is substantially more risky for the aliens.

2 PLAN AHEAD

You may not want to build an alien invasion bunker underneath your house but make sure you have that option – select a home on solid foundations with the right ground conditions for tunnelling. Avoid soft or damp areas and make use of any natural caves or man-made underground structures.

3 WHAT TO AVOID

Concentrated population centers are likely to become war zones in most alien invasion scenarios. Although you'll no doubt want to get into action in the service of humanity, select a home on the outskirts of town. Avoid proximity to any military bases, airports, power stations, or major communication hubs.

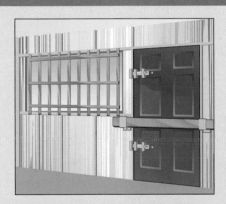

KEEPING A PET

It has been shown that dogs and cats seem to "notice" clones. It's by no means a 100% effective method but if your dog or cat goes crazy when someone enters, it's certainly worth trying to explore why.

The ASPCA has counselled against trying to put a small foil hat on a cat as this does leave felines exposed to alien mind-control techniques.

Dogs are generally the best anti-alien pets and will happily wear a stylish doggie foil cap. Several ET preppers in New England have successfully trained ferrets, with promising results.

THREAT 3
PHYSICAL THREAT

All forms of electronic locks, alarms, and other such defenses have proved to be ineffective against aliens attempting to break into a home. To stop an alien gaining entry into your home, think low technology. Use the strongest possible metal locks and bolts, and back these up by barricading all doors and windows with wooden beams. Have your walls treated with aluminium "wool" to prevent aliens from using their "walking through walls" dematerialization technologies.

THREAT 4
CLONE ATTACK

ET preppers often tick off many of the precautions already covered in this section, only to forget about the "soft" form of alien home invasion: the use of clones to implant devices around the home. Clones often pose as repair men or similar, so be aware of the activities and purpose of any unfamiliar persons entering your home and monitor their work while they're present. It's worth insisting on a clone check before anyone enters your property.

ABDUCTION PROOFING THE HOME

Preventing an alien abduction not only avoids the considerable physical and mental stress such hostile action places on the person in question, but it also strikes a blow against any extraterrestrial plans for humanity. It's widely understood that the Grays are responsible for most abductions and their primary motivation is the monitoring and collection of DNA and biological matter. However, there are some who believe that they're also probing for weaknesses in species. They may be seeking to develop a virus or bio-weapon to turn us into passive slaves – we just can't be sure. Making your home more resistant to abduction attempts is a good start.

Don't overlook the core structure of your home or apartment. A standard brick or wooden structure will be unable to take much punishment so, if you have the funds, invest in a reinforced concrete support framework to underpin the building. Sometimes older homes are more robust than newer ones.

STEP 1
DOORS AND WINDOWS

Aliens from a landed ship will make use of any easy access point, much as any intruder would. Despite all the high-tech tricks possessed by these unwelcome visitors, however, they have one significant weakness that we can exploit. Aliens struggle with wooden obstructions: this may sound low-tech to us but many of these civilizations stopped used organic woods thousands of years ago. Install wooden latches – not metal ones – on all doors and windows, and hold things together by means of wooden dowels rather than metal screws, bolts, or nails. Wooden shutters across windows are effective at resisting alien technology and, of course, can look rather picturesque, giving your home that "French rustic" look in summer.

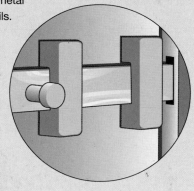

Try lining the walls with foil at night to avoid suspicion

STEP 2
EXTERNAL WALLS

Where you have cavity walls, these can be filled with standard insulating foam provided it has been mixed with aluminium or iron filings. It's also recommended that a thick sheet of foil be tacked to the walls – the foil can then be painted or wallpapered over. If you have solid walls, a thicker lining is preferable – at least three layers of metallic sheet.

STEP 3
ROOF AND CEILING

For about the same price as it costs to insulate your attic, you can alien-proof your roof and ceiling, giving you the peace of mind of knowing that alien mind probes and tractor beams won't easily shoot through. The standard solution involves layers of metallic foil underneath your roof tiles and inside the roof lining, stapled to the joists and rafters. Ensure that you use extra-thick industrial-strength aluminium foil. Aluminium foil attic insulation can be purchased at any DIY store and can also help reduce risk of condensation and penetrating damp – a win-win situation. Finally, put a layer of slate or lead across the attic floor for additional protection.

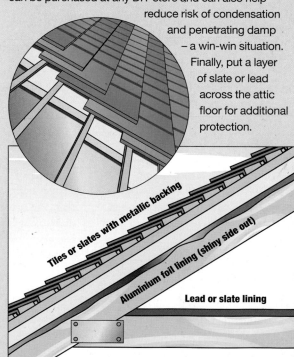

Tiles or slates with metallic backing

Aluminium foil lining (shiny side out)

Lead or slate lining

▶ BUILD YOUR OWN ALIEN SAFE ROOM

Where budgetary or time constraints restrict your alien defense preparations, you may wish to convert one room into an alien safe room. Even if you've alien-proofed other parts of the home, it's still useful to have a secure location where you and your family can dash if you hear the hum of a saucer. For those with a very limited budget, it's possible to convert a small wardrobe or cupboard into an alien survival pod – which is similar to a safe room but much smaller.

AT THE FIRST SIGN OF TROUBLE...

You should get to your safe room as soon as possible. Ensure that you have essentials – blankets, water, and snacks – in your safe room as you should ideally stay there for at least four hours. Practice with your family to ensure that everyone can get to your safe room in less than 30 seconds. Once inside, seal the doors and don't be tempted to leave until you're absolutely sure that any hovering ships have left.

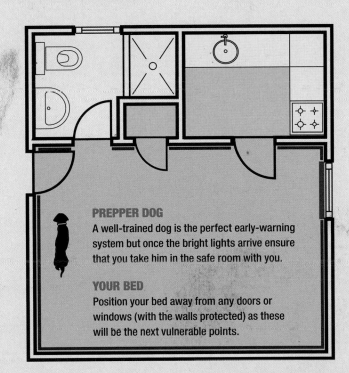

INTERNAL DOOR
Door is fitted with wooden dead-bolts and wooden fastenings to fix it to the wall – don't let ET use his sonic screwdriver to undo the hinges only to see the door drop to the floor!

SAFE ROOM
A well-stocked alien safe room, with thick lead and aluminium lining, and 24 hours' worth of food and water. Keep a few good books in there as well.

INTERNAL WALLS
Walls treated with aluminium-based foam and foil; this prevents alien "wall-walking" and provides a practical base layer for painting or wallpapering.

PREPPER DOG
A well-trained dog is the perfect early-warning system but once the bright lights arrive ensure that you take him in the safe room with you.

YOUR BED
Position your bed away from any doors or windows (with the walls protected) as these will be the next vulnerable points.

WINDOWS
Windows may be left clear during the day but a silver-foil blind is pulled down at night to prevent alien mind-control waves filtering in. The window is also fitted with wooden bolts.

CONSIDERING A NEW HOME?
If you're planning to move, ensure that you audit your next location against the information and advice provided in this guide. If in any doubt, ask your real estate agent or the vendor about any anti-abduction features of the property.

NO HOME CAN BE TOTALLY ABDUCTION-RESISTANT BUT THE IMPROVEMENTS DESCRIBED HERE CAN REDUCE THE RISK OF ALIEN ABDUCTION BY OVER 70%.

⚠ WARNING

FOR STRUCTURAL WORK ON YOUR HOME, SUCH AS THE MOVING OF WALLS OR THE DIGGING OF AN ALIEN DEFENSE BUNKER, CONSULT THE LOCAL AUTHORITIES. IF YOU'RE RENTING, YOU NEED TO LET THE LANDLORD KNOW ABOUT YOUR CONCERNS. THE GOVERNMENT IS LOOKING TO INTRODUCE AN "ET SCHEME" IN WHICH HOME OWNERS CAN APPLY FOR GRANTS OF UP TO $5,000 TO IMPROVE ALIEN-PROOFING AROUND THE HOUSE.

THE PERFECT ALIEN INVASION BUNKER

So far we've looked at reasonably priced improvements you can make to your home to help you resist alien abduction or raids – lead lining will prevent the beaming out of your unconscious body, reflective foil will restrict an alien's ability to scan your home, and your alien survival pod may buy you some precious minutes if species such as the Grays or Little Green Men search your home. However, once an alien invasion starts, everything changes. For now it's enough to know that invasion will involve a variety of assaults from orbital bombardments and attacks from alien ships to a full-scale ground invasion and even a war of extermination.

BASICALLY, WE'RE SAYING THAT FOR A MAJOR ALIEN INVASION OF EARTH, YOU'RE GOING TO HAVE TO START THINKING MUCH BIGGER THAN A FEW EXTRA ROLLS OF FOIL. THE ULTIMATE SET-UP WOULD INCLUDE THE CREATION OF A FULLY FUNCTIONING BUNKER COMPLEX.

▶ ALIEN INVASION BUNKER

1 Construction should be concealed. In a military invasion by aliens, the bunker will become a center of resistance and intelligence.

2 It's recommended that a layer of lead and slate at least 4 inches (10cm) thick be laid over the top of the bunker. Alien scanners can detect underground structures but we know that this combination disrupts their readings.

3 The bunker should be equipped for your immediate needs but take into account that in the first week of an alien invasion you'll be joining up with other survivors to form an anti-invasion militia. Some of these survivors will come with their own weapons and bug-out bags.

4 A fully equipped medical bay to support a growing band of human resistance fighters.

5 Garrison bunk beds. There will be little privacy once your forces start to build up. Expect to have beds for at least 100 – by using "hot bunking" this will mean that you can operate a force of 200 fighters as you take the war to the aliens.

6 You will need a well-equipped workshop for repairs to equipment and weapons. Make sure that you include a library of military and survival books.

7 It's good to have a secure examination room and a few cells. If you manage to capture one of the invaders you may be able to extract valuable information. Even alien bodies can be useful as human forces need to know how any invaders tick biologically – what are their vulnerable areas?

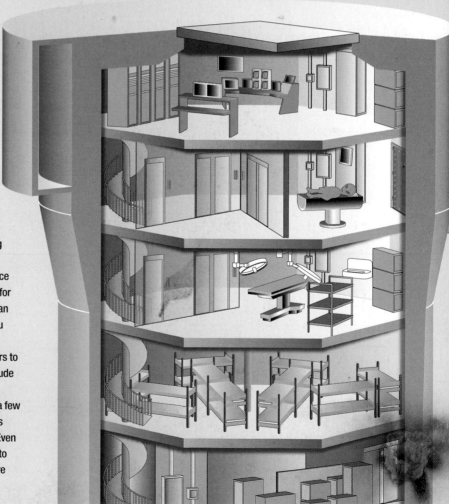

It may be worth creating a dummy site – maybe with an exposed concrete bunker top and an antenna or satellite dish sticking up. Don't overdo it – the purpose is just to be a distraction. If it's spotted by an alien patrol, hopefully this will be the site they attack first, giving you a chance to go into lock-down.

Call the township on Monday – I need a home with a bunker

11 Radio Free Earth – while your communications center will be abuzz with updates from missions in the field, contact with military units and any surviving government, the most important desk by far is the Radio Free Earth one – which broadcasts regularly to all survivors. You may need a more powerful system for this station to ensure that you can really reach out to people. As survivors cower in their homes while their towns and cities are destroyed by marauding tripods or unstoppable flying saucers, this voice will keep their hopes alive.

8 Command Room – this secure room should have a guard at all times and will quickly become the hub of any human resistance in the area. You'll need excellent maps of the local region; get large-scale maps and several of them. Ensure that you have maps of all underground infrastructure such as sewage tunnels or transport networks; any underground routes will be invaluable as the aliens can be expected to have air supremacy very early on. Humanity is going to need every advantage possible.

9 Conference Room – space to train your fighters, to update them on developments on the war, to debrief missions, and to start organizing the strike-back.

10 Communications Room – at the heart is a CB radio communications station, which can broadcast within a ten-mile (16-km) radius to human resistance fighters, any remaining military forces and other survivors. It's believed that going "low tech" will increase the chances of hiding the signals from any alien intervention.

12 CB antennae – a number of antennae should be hidden in various locations. It's vital that you keep broadcasting. As civilization is shattered, humanity will become disparate, with military forces breaking down into smaller units and an outbreak of general lawlessness. Remember, any informative broadcast can really help to galvanize survivors and create a focal point for the resistance. Encourage the populace to call in with reports of any alien activity.

GLOSSARY

ABDUCTION Taking someone away from a place by force.

BIOMATTER Plant material, vegetation, or agricultural waste used as a fuel or energy source; matter of biological origin; living or dead tissue.

CARTOUCHE An ornate or ornamental frame; an oval or oblong figure (as on ancient Egyptian monuments) enclosing a sovereign's name.

CLONE A plant or animal that is grown from one cell of its parent and that has exactly the same genes as its parent; a person or thing that appears to be an exact copy of another person or thing.

CONSPIRACY A secret plan made by two or more people to do something that is harmful or illegal; the act of secretly planning to do something that is harmful or illegal.

COVERT Made, shown, or done in a way that is not easily seen or noticed; secret or hidden.

DISPARATE Containing or made up of fundamentally different and often incongruous elements; markedly distinct in quality or character.

EXTRATERRESTRIAL Coming from or existing outside the planet Earth; originating, existing, or occurring outside the earth or its atmosphere.

GALVANIZE To cause (people) to become so excited or concerned about an issue, idea, etc., that they want to do something about it; to cause (a force that is capable of causing change) to become active.

HYBRID An offspring of two animals or plants of different breeds, varieties, species, or genera.

IMPLANT To put (something) in a specified place; to place (something) in a person's body by means of surgery; to cause (something) to become a part of the way a person thinks or feels.

INFRASTRUCTURE The basic equipment and structures (such as roads and bridges) that are needed for a country, region, or organization to function properly; the underlying foundation or basic framework (as of a system or organization); the permanent installations required for military purposes; the system of public works of a country, state, or region; the resources (as personnel, buildings, or equipment) required for an activity.

INTERGALACTIC Existing or occurring between galaxies; situated in or relating to the spaces between galaxies; of, relating to, or occurring in outer space.

INTERVENTION An interference with the outcome or course, especially of a condition or process (as to prevent harm or improve functioning).

MATRIX Something within or from which something else originates, develops, or takes form.

MENACE A dangerous or possibly harmful person or thing; someone who causes trouble or annoyance; a dangerous or threatening quality.

SPECIES A class of individuals having common attributes and designated by a common name; a logical division of a genus or more comprehensive class; a category of biological classification ranking immediately below the genus or subgenus, comprising related organisms or populations potentially capable of interbreeding.

STATISTIC A number that represents a piece of information (such as information about how often something is done, how common something is, etc.); a quantity (as the mean of a sample) that is computed from a sample.

SUPREMACY The quality or state of having more power, authority, or status than anyone else; the state of being supreme.

TELEPATHY A way of communicating thoughts directly from one person's mind to another person's mind without using words or signals; communication from one mind to another by extrasensory means.

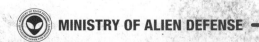

FOR MORE INFORMATION

National Aeronautics and Space Administration (NASA)
NASA Headquarters
300 E Street SW, Suite 5R30
Washington, DC 20546
(202) 358-0001
Website: http://www.nasa.gov
NASA's vision: To reach for new heights and reveal the unknown for the benefit of humankind. To do that, thousands of people have been working around the world—and off of it—for more than 50 years, trying to answer some basic questions. What's out there in space? How do we get there? What will we find? What can we learn there, or learn just by trying to get there, that will make life better here on Earth?

SETI Institute (Search for Extraterrestrial Intelligence)
189 Bernardo Avenue, Suite 100
Mountain View, CA 94043
Website: http://www.seti.org
The SETI Institute's mission is to explore, understand, and explain the origin and nature of life in the universe, and to apply the knowledge gained to inspire and guide present and future generations. We have a passion for discovery, and for sharing knowledge as scientific ambassadors to the public, the press, and the government.

Space Telescope Science Institute (STScI)
3700 San Martin Drive
Baltimore, MD 21218
(410) 338-4700
Website: http://www.stsci.edu/portal/
STScI is a free-standing science center, located on the campus of The Johns Hopkins University and operated by the Association of Universities for Research in Astronomy (AURA) for NASA. It operates the science program for the Hubble Space Telescope and will conduct the science and mission operations for the James Webb Space Telescope and supports other astronomy programs and conducts world-class scientific research.

SpaceX
Rocket Road
Hawthorne, CA
(310) 363-6000
Website: http://www.spacex.com
SpaceX designs, manufactures, and launches advanced rockets and spacecraft. The company was founded in 2002 to revolutionize space technology, with the ultimate goal of enabling people to live on other planets. It is the only private company ever to return a spacecraft from low-Earth orbit. In 2012, its Dragon spacecraft attached to the International Space Station, exchanged cargo payloads, and returned safely to Earth — a technically challenging feat previously accomplished only by governments. Since then Dragon has delivered cargo to and from the space station multiple times, providing regular cargo resupply missions for NASA. SpaceX will fly numerous cargo resupply missions to the ISS, and, in the near future, SpaceX will carry crew as well. Currently under development is the Falcon Heavy, which will be the world's most powerful rocket. All the while, SpaceX continues to work toward one of its key goals—developing reusable rockets, a feat that will transform space exploration by delivering highly reliable vehicles at radically reduced costs.

WEBSITES

Because of the changing nature of Internet links, Rosen Publishing has developed an online list of Web sites related to the subject of this book. This site is updated regularly. Please use this link to access this list:

http://www.rosenlinks.com/SACW/contact

FOR FURTHER READING

Aguilar, David A. *Alien Worlds: Your Guide to Extraterrestrial Life.* Des Moines, IL: National Geographic Children's Books, 2013.

Asimov, Isaac. *Extraterrestrial Civilizations.* New York, NY: Ballantine Books, 2011.

Brake, Mark. *Alien Life Imagined: Communicating the Science of Astrobiology.* New York, NY: Cambridge University Press, 2012.

Friedman, Stanton T. *UFOs: Real or Imagined?.* New York, NY: Rosen Publishing, 2011.

Friedman, Stanton T., and Kathleen Marden. *True Stories of Alien Abduction.* New York, NY: Rosen Publishing, 2014.

Leivsson, Eirik. *UFOs and Aliens: Exceptional Cases of Alien Contact.* Seattle, WA: CreateSpace, 2016.

Petrikowski, Nicki Peter. *A New Frontier: The Past, Present, and Future Search for Extraterrestrial Life.* New York, NY: Rosen Publishing, 2016).

Pye, Michael, and Kirsten Dalley. *Lost Cities and Forgotten Civilizations.* New York, NY: Rosen Publishing, 2012).

Scarsi, Andrea. *Extraterrestrial Channeling: Alien Abduction Syndrome.* Seattle, WA: CreateSpace, 2016.

Von Ward, Paul. *We've Never Been Alone: A History of Extraterrestrial Intervention.* Newburyport, MA: Hampton Roads Publishing, 2011.

Webb, Stuart. *Alien Encounters.* New York, NY: Rosen Publishing, 2012.

Webb, Stuart. *UFOs.* New York, NY: Rosen Publishing, 2012.

INDEX

A
Area 51, 9, 10, 11, 14

B
British Roswell, 13, 14

C
cartouche, 5
cattle mutilation, 28, 29
clones, 5, 14, 15, 23, 32, 33, 36, 38
cloning, 16, 26, 27, 29
communication, alien, 17, 19

D
DNA manipulation, 16, 27
Draconians, 4, 6, 7, 12, 16, 18, 20, 23, 25, 26, 29, 34
   "Smiley," 26, 27, 31
   vessels of, 14, 15
Dulce Airbase, 4, 10, 11, 12, 13, 22

E
ET Invasion Matrix, 15
ET preppers, 16, 17, 22, 30
   becoming one, 32, 34, 35, 36, 38, 40, 41, 42, 44
   products for, 38–39
extraterrestrial activity, history of, 4, 5, 7

G
Grays, 4, 8, 11, 12, 13, 14, 18, 19, 20, 22, 23, 25, 26, 28, 34, 36, 42, 44
   hybrid experiments with, 6
   saucers of, 8–9, 10, 24, 40

H
home defense, 40–44
hybridization, 5, 6, 9, 10, 13, 39

I
implants, 4, 16, 17, 24, 25, 26, 27, 29, 31, 39, 41
   Draconian, 27
   of ideas, 34
   removal of, 27
intergalactic accords, 20
intervention, alien, 4, 6, 14, 15, 30, 40, 45
invasion, alien, 4, 5, 14, 15, 16, 17, 22, 30, 31, 32, 33, 34, 35, 36, 37, 38, 40, 41
   bunker for, 44

L
Little Green Men, 4, 8, 9, 10, 12, 14, 15, 16, 20, 23, 31, 40, 44

M
Men in Black, 4, 10, 15, 18, 20, 21, 23

N
Nazis, 8, 9
Nordics, 18, 19, 20, 23, 38

P
post-Roswell era, 4, 14

R
Roswell crash, 4, 8, 11

T
Treaty of Greada, 4, 11, 14

U
UFO sightings, 4, 8, 14, 15, 16, 21, 31
UN Office for Earth Defense, 4, 15, 16, 18, 21, 39